<u>100</u>
<u>Neo-Futurist</u>
<u>Plays</u>

Written by

Greg Allen   Scott Hermes
Dave Awl   Spencer Kayden
Lisa Buscani   Greg Kotis
Karen Christopher   Tim Reinhard
Betsy Freytag   Phil Ridarelli
Ayun Halliday   Heather Riordan

From

"Too Much Light Makes The Baby Go Blind" ®
(30 Plays in 60 Minutes ®)

Created by

Greg Allen

CHICAGO
PLAYS

CHICAGO PLAYS, INC.
2632 N. LINCOLN
CHICAGO, IL 60614

PREFACE

You hold in your hand a book called **100 Neo-Futurist Plays from "Too Much Light Makes the Baby Go Blind."** You may wonder how, in fact, a hundred plays managed to slip into such a thin volume. And then you notice the subtitle: "30 Plays In 60 Minutes" and you brilliantly arrive at the conclusion that these are *very short plays*. "Why not call them scenes," you might well ask, "or even skits?" Because (the obvious answer) they are not. They are plays. And we are adamant about this point.

You see, we, the Neo-Futurists - like our namesakes the Italian Futurists and their relative contemporaries the Dadaists and the German Expressionists (to say nothing of the likes of Samuel Beckett, Kenneth Koch, and Howard Barker) - believe that you can, in fact, write a two-minute play with just as much depth and humor and poignancy as something that takes five acts, twenty characters, fifteen set changes, and two hours and ten minutes to complete. Perhaps - dare we say it? - we can achieve even more.

Neo-Futurism is based on the concept that the more sincere and genuine the performers are on stage, the greater will be your identification with the unadorned people and issues before you. Hence, we embrace a form of non-illusory theater in order to present our lives and ideas as directly as possible. All of our plays are "set" on the stage in front of the audience. All of our "characters" are ourselves. All of our stories really happened. And all of our tasks are actual challenges. We do not aim to "suspend the audience's disbelief" but to create a world where the stage is a continuation of daily life.

This may all sound like a lot of high-falootin' theory coming from a late-night show, but as you read these plays think of them being performed by a bunch of people named Phil and Robin and Lisa jumping around on an empty set wearing street clothes. There's nothing here that requires any special pyrotechnics - just an occasional blackout, some candles, the guts to get nude, or the bladder capacity to drink an incredibly large quantity of water.

You'll note quite a number of plays with scenarios for audience interaction. Throughout the shows, the audience is encouraged to express their feelings about what is happening. In some instances plays are based around their willingness to participate, but often the environment is such that it just happens. Someone is offended by a line and lets fly with a pointed retort. Someone else comes to the conclusion that they need to walk on stage and rectify a situation, so they do. This is all embraced in the moment. There's no fourth wall here. The people in the seats are just as vital and important as the people on stage. And they know it.

To encourage us to reflect our current lives and experiences on stage as directly as possible, we also create between two and twelve new plays a week. Nothing ever gets the chance to become fully predictable. To date, we've created 1,296 plays (as I write this, we plan to premiere another eight new plays this Friday, January 22nd, 1993). That's enough for another dozen books (but we'll see how well this one sells first.)

-Greg Allen

Neo-Futurism has convinced me of the beauties of failure and fighting. The ever-changing nature of **Too Much Light Makes The Baby Go Blind** poses an invigorating creative challenge and explains the phenomenon of audience members returning 10, 20 even 50 times. It also provides a host of potential pitfalls and conflict.

"Time," as we continually remind the audience, "is of the essence!" - a maxim that can certainly be applied to the submission and selection of our weekly "menu" of plays. Inspiration is rarely a problem. The newspapers, the city streets, pop culture and, of course, our personal lives are rich sources of raw material, though frequently the demands of running a theatre and performing 'til the wee hours dictate that a good idea will not be scripted 'til the zero hour. Some of my best work has been scribbled on the bus from my day job to rehearsal. Can you tell which of the plays in this collection are "quickies"? Probably not. Participation in the ensemble exercises our creative muscles to the point where I feel much of our writing is done instinctively, past experience leading us toward a style, tone or staging that will support the points we hope to make.

The fighting arises from the weekly system of cuts and proposals. Before new plays can be added to the menu, a certain number of old ones must go on the chopping block. Occasionally, a popular play is allowed to retire gracefully. More often, a play falls victim to circumstance, sometimes dying an untimely death simply because the subject matter is suddenly obsolete. The lightening quick dissolution of the Soviet Union outmoded a good portion of that week's menu in the few days between rehearsal and performance. Some plays evade the executioner by sheer circumstance. I can think of several dozen excessively "thin" plays that survived well past their shelf life just because they were short.

Having no single authority figure to decide a play's fate, it falls to the author to defend an old play from its attackers, to convince the nonbelievers that a lackluster proposal contains the seeds of genius. I have noticed that the newest ensemble members are always the most gracious in submitting to the group will. As they season into hoary old hands, they think nothing of going to the mat in stunning displays of viciousness. Strong objections necessitate lengthy, often heated discussion in which the Neo-Futurists try to predict the audience's response to the proposed play. Is it possible that the audience will misinterpret our attempts at satire or open-ended subtlety and assume that we are racists, homophobes, sexists or Republicans? Should we care if they do? We go 'round and 'round on this issue.

One of the most deflating criticisms is that a play is operating outside the Neo-Futurist aesthetic, a set of guidelines which, while easy to grasp in the abstract, can become a bit slippery when applied to specific cases. Given the fact that we always play ourselves, it is obviously non-Neo-Futurist for one of us to play, say, a Viet Nam veteran, but what if we merely give voice to the words of a Viet Nam veteran, making no attempt to vocally, physically or psychologically impersonate a character? We once solved this problem by announcing, "Adrian is not a Viet Nam veteran" at the top of a play in which Adrian and Karen recreated a conversation Karen had had on a plane with a panicky vet. Voila! The Neo-Futurist Aesthetic is upheld!

We've written over a thousand plays. They're not all gems. Any given performance is likely to include a dud or two, well-intentioned but flawed or perhaps just plain stupid. Each of us has spawned at least one play that is so horrendous, its very title evokes cringing. You won't find them in this collection; nonetheless, they are valuable for the courageousness they cultivate.

How do we keep it up, how do we find the stamina to come up with the goods on a weekly basis? I know I had to adjust some of my attitudes about perfection. The fact is that the world will not explode if I forget the lines I learned on Tuesday or fumble with a prop. The important thing is to acknowledge the unscheduled turn of events, tell the audience, "Yes, I'm aware of what just happened. No doubt you are, too, seeing as how we're in the same room."

We can write plays and see them fail, go down in flames, stink to high heaven and accept that failure as a necessary life force of Neo-Futurism. Once I realized that not every play is golden, I was able to experiment more, deviate from the narrow realm of things I am good at in order to test different waters. And sometimes those different waters have spit up gems.

We are very lucky as writers to have immediate response to our work on such a consistent basis. Neo-Futurism is not a casual hobby. I'm incredibly fortunate to be mixed up in it.

-Ayun Halliday

INTRODUCTION

Obviously, **Too Much Light Makes the Baby Go Blind** has a long and multifaceted history which it would be particularly un-Neo-Futurist to go into at length. But, for the sake of history, here's the quick version:

I began to dicker around with performing Italian Futurist plays while at Oberlin College. I formed a group called "The Automatons" comprised of myself, Kate Goehring, Blair Thomas (both of whom have since become very prominent Chicago theater artists), John Russell, and Kirk Van Scoyoc. We mounted a collection of Italian Futurist plays and, suffice it to say, they went over like gangbusters. Skip a few years to find Greg in Chicago feeling frustrated at being unable to write the great American play. I hit on the idea of writing three scenarios or scripts every day as fast as I possibly could on one page of notebook paper. These were then performed at a staged reading at The Organic Theater's Greenhouse under the collective title **Too Much Light Makes The Baby Go Blind** and the gang-buster response was repeated.

Skip another year and I was presented with the opportunity to direct anything I wanted to as a late-night/off-night at Stage Left Theater. I decided the most frightening thing I could imagine was to form an ensemble to fool around with the Futurist stuff and the three-to-a-page scenario format and present it all under the aegis of **30 Plays in 60 Minutes**. I managed to coerce eight people to go along with me and I quickly set about to instill in them all the fire and brimstone of the performance theory I had gradually developed (and become obsessed with) over the last few years. I called it Neo-Futurism.

After five weeks of rehearsal we had prepared and created nearly fifty pieces (some were adaptations of original Italian Futurist plays) and threw thirty of them up for public consumption on December 2nd, 1988 under the collective title **Too Much Light Makes The Baby Go Blind**. The experience of the audience members was designed to approximate the chaos of the outside world. They paid a random admission ($1 times the roll of a single six-sided die), were each slapped with an erroneous name tag by a Walkman-wearing host, and forced on stage and questioned about their lives by the ensemble. Only then could they sit in their traditional seats - never again to even possibly consider that this show was anything akin to "Cats." The performance began with an incendiary Neo-Futurist manifesto I delivered off the top of my head and then, after a countdown, we started an on-stage 60 minute darkroom timer. Each play began with an emphatic "Go!" and ended with a shouted "Curtain!" That opening night we happily finished the last play with 94 seconds left on the clock.

As the show plunged on into 1989 and "the Bush era," I felt that rather than performing the plays from a set list, a random order was more consistent with Neo-Futurism. Each audience member was given "menus" with the titles of the plays to be performed that night, numbered one through thirty. These corresponded to numbers on a clothesline which crossed the stage. The audience was instructed to "order by number" and I would jump up and pluck down the next play to be performed. This succeeded in inspiring audience interaction and guaranteed us an unexpected, unrepeatable show.

As the weeks rolled along, we rapidly built a following that kept coming back with new friends to see new material each week. The show sold out for the first time June 10th, finally got some media attention with an article in the Chicago Tribune in November, and then sold out continuously for two years beginning in December of 1989. In May of 1990 we moved the show to the Live Bait Theatre. Finally on Valentine's Day, 1992 we moved into our own Neo-Futurarium, with our 1000th play. February 25th, 1993, **Too Much Light Makes The Baby Go Blind** made its Off-Broadway premiere at The Joseph Papp Public Theater in New York. Sometime in August of 1993 we published this book. And today you picked it up and are reading this sentence. After that... well, we'll just have to see, won't we?

- Greg Allen, 1993

The following is a list of everyone who has ever performed the show followed by their dates of performance. Each one of these people put their life and soul on stage and without them "Too Much Light Makes The Baby Go Blind" would not exist today:

Greg Allen	Dec. 2, 1988 -
Randy Burgess	Dec. 2, 1988 - April 28, 1990
Phil Gibbs	Dec. 2, 1988 - April 23, 1989
Rex Jenny	Dec. 2, 1988 - Jan. 28, 1989
Kathy Keyes	Dec. 2, 1988 - April 15, 1989
Melissa Lindberg	Dec. 2, 1988 - April 28, 1990
Robin MacDuffie	Dec. 2, 1988 - Dec. 2, 1989
Mike Troccoli	Dec. 2, 1988 - Sept. 9, 1989
Sheri Reda	Feb. 3, 1989 - July 9, 1989
Karen Christopher	April 14, 1989 -
Lisa Buscani	April 28, 1989 - Dec. 13, 1992
Alexis Smith	May 12, 1989 - June 24, 1989
Phil Ridarelli	May 18, 1989 -
Ted Bales	Dec. 8, 1989 - Dec. 21, 1991
Adrian Danzig	Dec. 8, 1989 - July 21, 1990
Ayun Halliday	Dec. 8, 1989 -
Page Phillips	Dec. 8, 1989 - April 21, 1990
Dave Awl	June 29, 1990 -
Spencer Kayden	June 29, 1990 -
Heather Riordan	July 6, 1990 -
Betsy Freytag	March 15, 1991 - March 7, 1993
Tim Reinhard	May 10, 1991 - June 6, 1992
Greg Kotis	May 24, 1991 -
Scott Hermes	Sept. 25, 1992 -
Diana Slickman	Jan. 8, 1993 -
Lusia Strus	Jan. 8, 1993 -
David Kodeski	Feb. 12, 1993 -
Anita Loomis	March 10, 1995 -
Stephanie Shaw	March 10, 1995

Contents

THE ACCELERATION OF A FALLING BODY IS 9.8 METERS PER SECOND PER SECOND
©1990 by Spencer Kayden

(Spencer holds a fishing pole. A feather is attached to the end of the line which she reels in throughout the play.)

SPENCER.
If shame and this feather
Were dropped
From the top of potential
It is said they will fall
At the same velocity
Although I can't imagine
They will hit the ground at the
Same time.
You promise they will as you
Dangle them over the ledge of perhaps.
My neck aches in constant anticipation
As I watch your experiment
Anxiously from below.
It is only when I use my
Unbeguiling binoculars
That I can see how angry
Your knuckles are.
What kind of lengthy preparation
Is required that takes you
So very long
To release the feather I plucked
From expectation and the shame
I carved from my gut.
As I watch your experiment
Anxiously from below.
It is only when I use my
Unbeguiling binoculars
That I can see how angry
Your knuckles are.
And I beg you to drop them
But my voice is carried away
By the wind of common practice
And by the time my message
Reaches you it sounds like
A love letter.

CURTAIN

ACCOMMODATING EXCLUSION
©1991 by Spencer Kayden

(All are singing a Christian choral tune. Tim is conducting. After a few measures Spencer and Greg K. are audibly discussing something.)

ALL.
What a friend we have in Jesus
All our sins & grief to bear
What a privilege to carry
Everything to God in prayer
(Tim stops the singing and confronts Greg K. and Spencer.)
TIM. Excuse me, are we interrupting you?
GREG K. No, sorry.
TIM. May we begin again?
(Singing commences. Spencer and Greg K. talk more.)
TIM. Spencer, would you like to share with the rest of the group what is so important?
SPENCER. I was asking Greg if it bugged him to sing about Jesus our Savior.
TIM. And Greg said?
GREG K. I said I was just singing. It's just a song.
SPENCER. Yeah, but Greg and I are Jewish.
TIM. So you don't have to sing.
GREG K. *(to Spencer.)* No one is forcing us to sing.
TIM. Feel free to sit this play out. No one said you had to be in it.
SPENCER. No one said we had to sing this song.
TIM. Yes but this is the song we're singing. And I have already told you, you have the choice to sing it or not.
SPENCER. So it's either sing this song or not sing at all.
TIM. It's entirely your decision. No one is making you sing.
TED. Can we get on with this.
PHIL. It's hot in here.
BETSY. I'm thirsty.
GREG A. I'm hungry.
AYUN. What kind of pizza did we get?
SPENCER. Pepperoni.
HEATHER. But I'm a vegetarian.
SPENCER. *(Pause.)* So you don't have to eat it.
(Pause. Start song.)
ALL.
What a friend we have in Jesus
All our sins and grief to bear
What a privilege to carry
Everything to God in prayer.

CURTAIN

AD NAUSEAM
©1989 by Greg Allen

(An off-stage voice calls out "Act One" as Greg Allen and Phil Gibbs walk on from stage left. They are very nervous.)

GREG. Well ... I had a nice time.
PHIL. Yeah, ... it was ... um ...
GREG. It was fun.
PHIL. Yeah, it was nice. It was fun.
(They laugh and fidget uncomfortably.)
PHIL. Well, ... uh ... I gotta go.
GREG. Yeah, it's late.
PHIL. I'll ... I'll see you around.
GREG. Yeah, ... I'll see you.
PHIL. Goodnight.
GREG. Bye.

(Phil and Greg exit in opposite directions. The offstage voice calls out "Act One". Greg and Phil enter from either side of the stage and repeat the previous scene as exactly as possible, exiting the same ways again. The off stage voice calls out "Act One" and Greg and Phil enter for another repetition. This continues ad nauseam until someone in the audience offers them a solution to their predicament. When a solution is offered, Greg and Phil try to go with it as honestly as possible and then the curtain is called.)

CURTAIN

THE AT-HOME-BIG-BUDGET-ACTION-FLICK KIT
(NO COUPONS OR PASSES ACCEPTED)
©1991 by Phil Ridarelli and Jim Kelly

(Phil stands before the audience holding a shoebox.)

PHIL. My favorite Christmas gift? Why, my At-Home-Big-Budget-Action-Flick Kit, of course. It comes with everything I need to make my own big budget action flick right in the comfort of my own living room. Oh, sure, I know you're probably thinking, "Gee, Phil, these blood-soaked pseudo-epics cranked out by Hollywood assembly lines do nothing but diminish the value of human life." Sure, but what a lot of cool explosions for just seven bucks! Let's see what's in it.
(Phil looks through the shoe box.)
A pack of cigarettes, of course. The hero smokes a lot, but he's in great shape. A pair of cool sunglasses to be used along with the cigarettes in order to create that hip action flick attitude. It says here that sunglasses are optional and squinting may be substituted.
(Heather enters and stands beside Phil.)
Oh, and look, I got my very own wife-slash-girlfriend to give my character some depth. She's only to be used twice in our action flick. Once early in the film to establish my sense of inner conflict...
HEATHER. You love the force more than your own wife. *(She slaps him.)*
PHIL. ...and then again at the end of our flick, after the big fight scene, to show that I've resolved all my personal issues.
HEATHER. Oh, baby, I love you.
(She embraces him.)
PHIL. Oh, and look, a memento of my troubled past! In this case a newspaper clipping. This will be really important later on when I have to confront my troubled past in order to kill the... oh boy! A millionaire bad guy with an accent! They come in either overweight or balding.
(Greg Allen enters as the bad guy.)
PHIL. Mine's balding!
GREG A. Kill him.
PHIL. It says here that some of the more sophisticated viewers may notice the subtle homo-erotic relationship between myself and the bad guy.
GREG A. I must admit, I admire your tenacity.
GREG. K. Hey, Phil, look! It's a car chase!
(Greg K. pulls the Tyco Super Cliff-Hanger Nite-Glo race track into view.)
PHIL. Excellent! I can't wait to use it. Hey, look, you guys! My very own action flick gun! It only runs out of ammo when I'm ready to reload.
KAREN. Hey, Phil, you dropped this out of your kit.
PHIL. What is it?
KAREN. It's your "Create your own signature tag line" mad lib.
PHIL. Great! Let's put it together.
KAREN. Well, Phil, first we need a verb pertaining to one of your senses.
(They elicit responses from the audience.)
KAREN. Now we need an article of clothing.
(They get responses.)

KAREN. Well, Phil, it looks as though your signature tag line is, *"(Touch)* my *(socks),* sucker!"

PHIL. *"(touch)* my *(socks),* sucker!"* Hey, I like it! Well, guys, whatta ya say we make an action flick?

GREG K. Phil's big budget action flick! Action!

(Phil now has sunglasses on and is smoking a cigarette.)

HEATHER. You love the force more than your own wife.

(She slaps him. He stares at the newspaper clipping.)

GREG A. Kill him.

(They fight over the bad guy's gun. It falls to the floor. They run to the race track and begin racing the cars. When one flies off the tracks, they run to Phil's gun and fight over it. They stop.)

GREG A. I must admit, you have a beautiful body.

(They resume fighting. Greg A. falls.)

PHIL. *(Touch)* my *(socks),* sucker!

(Phil shoots the bad guy, runs out of bullets. Greg A. is relieved. Magically the gun is reloaded and Phil resumes shooting. Greg dies.)

HEATHER. Oh, baby, I love you.

(She embraces him. Phil crumples the newspaper clipping.)

CURTAIN

ATTRACTION
©1992 by Scott Hermes

(Lights out. Heather slowly circles Scott, inspecting him with a dimly lit flashlight.)

PHIL. What is it that i like about you
AYUN. why do i
SCOTT. why
GREG K. why do i do it
HEATHER. with you
GREG A. to you
PHIL. what is it that you do
AYUN. that i do
SCOTT. that we do
GREG K. why is it that you do that voodoo that you do so well
HEATHER. what is it that
GREG A. i like
PHIL. i like to like
AYUN. what is it that i touch
SCOTT. that
GREG K. i touch that
HEATHER. i touch that
GREG A. and
PHIL. i touch that
AYUN. and you
SCOTT. touch
GREG K. and we *(pause)*
HEATHER. what is it that you do do when you do that voodoo that you do to me
GREG A. how is it that you can do that
PHIL. to me
AYUN. with me
SCOTT. with me
GREG K. of all people why me, why me
HEATHER. why me
GREG A. why me worry? When you do that, i don't care what
PHIL. or why
AYUN. or where
SCOTT. just do that
GREG K. voodoo
HEATHER. you do
GREG A. so well
PHIL. well
AYUN. well, well, well, well, well.

CURTAIN

BAD AFFIRMATION
©1991 by Ayun Halliday

(Ayun sits center stage listening to a Walkman.)

AYUN. In the infinity of life where I am, all is perfect, whole, and complete. I am always divinely protected and guided - it is safe to look within myself. I am totally willing to learn to love myself.
(As Ayun speaks, Heather enters wearing Walkman headphones, notices Ayun, and plugs her earphones into the same Walkman Ayun is listening to.)
AYUN & HEATHER. I love my body. My body is the temple through which all life flows - My body can have whatever it wants. Everybody should want my body. I love my beautiful body.
(As Ayun and Heather speak, Dave enters with his own earphones, noticing and then joining Ayun as Heather did.)
AYUN, HEATHER, & DAVE. I will love and nurture my Inner Child. My inner child has been wounded. I will give my inner child everything it wants. I will seek out the people who wounded my Inner Child and kill them. My parents deserve to die.
(Spencer enters wearing her own headphones and joins Ayun, Heather, and Dave.)
AYUN, HEATHER, DAVE, & SPENCER. I am totally open to the abundant flow of prosperity within the Universe. I deserve to have whatever I want. I will begrudge my friends any good fortune that comes their way because they are assholes and should keep their hands off money which is rightfully mine!
(Tim enters with headphones. He joins the rest.)
AYUN, HEATHER, DAVE, SPENCER, & TIM. I am the Supreme Being of the universe! Anyone who doesn't realize that has his head jammed up his ass! I have been misunderstood, unappreciated, and lied to all my life, but now revenge is mine! *(Pause. Sigh.)* In the infinity of life where I am, all is perfect, whole and complete.

CURTAIN

BEAUTY AND THE BREAST
©1991 by Betsy Freytag

(Betsy, Heather, Karen, and Ayun stand facing the audience. They each wear lab coats.)

BETSY. We'd like to take this moment to share with you some insight into the female breast.

HEATHER. As young girls develop, having big breasts is extremely important.

KAREN. In puberty, young women twist and turn in front of mirrors, craning their necks in hopes of getting a glimpse of the first sign of "BREASTS".

AYUN. And they never come fast enough. In fact, every teenager at least contemplates stuffing her shirt with kleenex, sox, a piece of fruit...whatever it takes to compete with one's peers. As all young women know, "She who has sizable breasts..."

ALL. "...Wins."

KAREN. Well, the fact is, every female is born with the exact same number of nerve endings in her breasts.

AYUN. A "36 double D" cup has the same number as a "32 A".

BETSY. Therefore, the bigger the breasts, the farther apart the nerve endings. The farther apart the nerve endings, the more diluted the sensation. The less the sensation, the less the arousal. And the more you suck on them, the more bored I get. I mean my breasts are only a minute part of me...touch me, touch the whole woman! You'd probably get a bigger response out of me if you'd lick my elbow...

KAREN. Betsy!

BETSY. Oh shut up. What would you know about it. I bet you don't even own a bra, Miss Tender Titties. Oh, I'm sorry, I'm sorry... *(Ayun and Heather start to lead Betsy off.)* When I was thirteen, I felt something a couple of times...but now. *(To Heather)* Do you know what I mean? *(Looks at Heather's breasts)* Aw, you don't know what I mean... *(Ayun, Heather and Betsy exit, leaving Karen alone onstage. Heather reenters.)*

KAREN. Thank you for your time and attention.

CURTAIN

BLACK-EYED SUSANS
©1992 by Ayun Halliday

(Spencer kneels facing Ayun, who sits in a chair carefully smudging dark makeup around one of Spencer's eyes.)

AYUN. I saw three women with black eyes last week. Three different women, all out and about.
SPENCER. It's only makeup. It doesn't hurt.
AYUN. The first woman was shopping with her grown-up daughter at the Salvation Army. She was in a bad mood. She had a real shiner. It made me think of plums.
SPENCER. When this play is over, I'll go backstage and wipe it off. It only looks like it hurts.
AYUN. The second woman was working in a Filipino grocery. She asked where I had bought my dress. She was real curious about me, why I had come into her store when Jewel was right down the street. She had on frosted brown eyeshadow and lots of mascara and the bruise under her eye was starting to disperse in flecks of green and black and inky blue.
SPENCER. I don't have to worry. I know you're taking care not to hurt me. You even bought a special cream to take the color off. It won't sting me at all.
AYUN. The third woman was someone I actually know well enough to sympathize with about the trials of waitressing and the weather and why there's never enough time for everything. Ever. And it looked really bad from far away, but up close, I hardly noticed it at all. Funny, you'd think it'd be the other way around.
(Spencer stands, and faces the audience. One of her eyes is blackened with stage makeup. Ayun stands to face the back wall.)
SPENCER. What did you say?
AYUN. Excuse me, ma'am, is that your cart?
SPENCER. What did you say?
AYUN. This dress? I bought it at Clothestime. And it was really cheap.
SPENCER. What did you say?
AYUN. Okay, Margaret, see you in a few weeks.
SPENCER. This is beginning to sting a little. I want to wash it off.
AYUN. Okay.
(Spencer exits. Ayun sits to watch her leave.)

CURTAIN

BLONDELL
©1990 by Karen Christopher

(Karen, Robin, Greg A., and Melissa come on stage one at a time and start scrubbing the floor on their hands and knees. There are four performers' parts which are spoken in rounds, each performer starting a line behind the person in front of them.)

ALL.
I was talking to Blondell Cummings
Blondell is a choreographer
And Blondell is a dancer
And Blondell is black
And I said Blondell?
(Scrubbing stops one at a time as performers say "Blondell".)
KAREN.
Are you ever misunderstood?
(Scrubbing begins again.)
ALL.
Your work, I mean
Do people know how to read the signs
And do they know what to make of them?
And she said.
(Scrubbing stops.)
KAREN.
She said one time a critic came to see a show where she started the first piece out on her hands and knees washing the floor. The next day she read in the paper that she started the show as a cleaning lady washing someone's floor. The reviewer wished she'd been able to break away from the black, female maid stereotype. Well that idea had never occurred to her. She said...
(Each starts scrubbing on the next line.)
ALL.
I was washing... *(One after the other)*
KAREN.
My own damn floor.
ALL.
Whose floor did you think I was washing?
KAREN.
Whose floor did you think I was washing?

CURTAIN

BOIL THAT DUSTSPECK
©1990 by Ayun Halliday

(Ayun yawns and stretches. Phil and Greg Allen watch from a corner of the stage.)

PHIL. What a gorilla.
GREG. I know, can you believe she waits tables in those skimpy little outfits? It's enough to put you off your food.
PHIL. I would have to say it's a complete and utter turn-off.
GREG. You'd think she'd have enough self respect to spend a couple of minutes a day with a razor.
AYUN. What's that hair all over your face, buddy?!
GREG. My beard isn't unsanitary.
AYUN. Unsanitary. Right. A lot of people wonder why I stopped shaving my legs and under my arms. *(Heather and Spencer swing in on ropes yelling Tarzan-style.)*
AYUN. I get a lot of funny looks.
(Heather and Spencer squat contentedly.)
HEATHER & SPENCER. Ooka-chaka-laka-chaka. Ooka-chaka-laka-chaka.
AYUN. I used to shave.
HEATHER & SPENCER. Noooo!!!
AYUN. Once.
HEATHER & SPENCER. Ooka-chaka-laka-chaka. Ooka-chaka-laka-chaka.
AYUN. 'Til one day I was looking at my legs through a magnifying glass.
TED. Ooh, why were you doing that?!
AYUN. Don't know, just was - and I saw a tribe of little women...
HEATHER & SPENCER. Ooka-chaka-laka-chaka. Ooka-chaka-laka-chaka.
AYUN. Frolicking among the hairs.
DAVE. What were they up to?
HEATHER & SPENCER. Chattanooga!!! *(Heather and Spencer vigorously muss each other's hair while hopping around in circles.)*
AYUN. Fun, Dave, big fun. Life the way you'd like to live it, absolute undistilled communion with nature and self.
TED. So, what happened?
AYUN. I was late for the Prom. I took my Pink Daisy razor -
HEATHER & SPENCER. Nooo!!! *(Two men rush on and hack at Heather and Spencer with machetes. Heather and Spencer die in a flurry of red scarves.)*
AYUN. And shaved myself slick as a whistle, ankle to thigh!
TED. You wore a minidress to the Prom?
AYUN. No, a floor-length Gunne Sax that laced up the bodice, but that's not important. Anyways, a little while later I was looking through my magnifying glass...
DAVE. No, no, it's too horrible, I can't bear to hear it!
AYUN. And there were just bodies. Little hacked-apart severed bodies, lying in their own gore. They were so happy, once.
HEATHER & SPENCER. *(Returning to life)* Ooka-chaka-laka-chaka. Ooka-chaka-laka-chaka.
AYUN. But now they were dead, dead, mowed down by my own hand! And so I say to you, shaving women of the audience, men and women with a bias against any hair originating in a place other than head, eyebrow, or pubic region, examine yourselves. Take responsibility for ALL of your hair! AND STOP THE GENOCIDE NOW! *(Ayun strikes the "Evita" pose. Phil approaches her, ogling the hair in her armpit.)*
PHIL. Hey, Ayun. Can I touch it?

CURTAIN

CAB ADDICT
©1990 by Lisa Buscani

(Four chairs are set on stage in two rows. Lisa sits in the "back seat." Phil sits up front, driving.)

LISA:
The world is pushing,
the world is shoving,
the world is grasping for rung or pole,
the world is sharing sweat and breath,
the world is stepping-to-the-back-of-the-bus-please-people,
the world is closing in.
But not on me.
I am above the world.
I have chosen
(how I love that verb and its fat finality)
to take a cab.
Cabs make me automatically regal.
Someone out there somewhere
exists solely to serve me
and will whisk me
through the clogged arteries of our flabby metropolis
to a destination that no one else will share.
Fuck community,
I deserve curbside service.

Privacy is so soft,
so quiet.
The world of the cab is
a world of classical music on Sunday mornings,
the mouths of men after successful sex,
art museums during the Superbowl.
And the voice of the cab drivers
reflect and revere that intimacy
cheeks to pillow
cream to coffee.

PHIL:
Racine and Montrose?
Sure.
You know, it's supposed to snow . . .
Lips pillow day
Time sweet gift yellow hold . . .
you know?

LISA:
Yes . . .

PHIL:
So I says to the wife, I says . . .
"Dream brush wonder hug silhouette
Days kissing breath shiver silk.
Question cellophane dish and cream."
Am I right, or am I right?

LISA:
Yes, o-h-h y-e-e-e-s-s-s . . .

And as we glide through time,
the calm of it all is enough to consider,
just consider mind you,
moving to the suburbs.

CURTAIN

CATHY
©1991 by Ayun Halliday

(Ayun, Heather, and Phil stand on stage facing the audience.)

AYUN. Hi, I'm Cathy and I've brainwashed the majority of American women into thinking I'm the mouthpiece of their generation! Why, every day when I go shopping I can't help but see myself around every corner: Cathy greeting cards, Cathy calendars, Cathy coffee mugs to take to the office!

HEATHER. I'm Cathy's best friend, Andrea. In the old days, I used to chide her about her lack of feminist commitment, but then I was married off to some man with a lumpy butt -

AYUN. Everybody in this comic strip's got a lumpy butt! It's non-threatening! Plus, I've got stringy hair and dowdy clothes with hearts on them. No wonder women love me!

HEATHER. Now I'm forced to spew such nonsense as you can never be fulfilled as a woman unless you have a child. I never thought I'd sink so low.

PHIL. I'm Irving, Cathy's boyfriend. A couple of years ago, I was allowed to date other women and hang out with the guys, while Cathy sat by the phone spouting stupid metaphors about relationships.

AYUN. Relationships are like watching football on t.v. with your boyfriend after you've just eaten 14 lbs. of Halloween candy because all the new bathing suits at the mall are cut too high to cover your bulbous, lumpy ass!

PHIL. Now I'm listless and lazy and practically castrated, but does she shut up?

AYUN. If life is like a diet, how come I'm so fucking fat!?

(Dave enters wearing a short gray wig and an apron. He carries a bowl of cookies.)

DAVE. I'm Cathy's mom. Please Lord, don't make me wear this godforsaken apron for another day!

AYUN. CHOCOLATE CHIP COOKIES!!!

(Ayun dives headfirst into the bowl that Dave holds.)

DAVE. I will not comment on her weight, I will not hint about grandchildren, I will not ask if she's still a virgin even though she's well past thirty and you see Brenda Starr in sexual situations every single week while Cathy goes to bed with her teddy bear.

(Ayun looks up from the cookie bowl, makes the fat face.)

HEATHER. God, she's disgusting!

PHIL. What a pig!

DAVE. And yet...

AYUN. They love me! They're buying Cathy nightshirts and Cathy Post-It notes, even those butt-ugly Cathy dolls by the ton!

DAVE. I don't know how she does it.

AYUN. Suck on that, Snoopy!

CURTAIN

CENSOR
©1991 by Karen Christopher

(People on stage standing in a group, everyone is swaying erratically whenever Karen speaks. Karen is sitting in a chair in front of them.)

KAREN. I just cut my fingernails - again. I cut them last week and now I had to do it again. And I'm wondering how long, how long will this go on...

AYUN. Fuck this weather man, I can't take this heat.

GREG A. Get off this stage. I've had it with your obscenity, you are no longer allowed to speak.

AYUN. Who gives you the right?

GREG A. Look, no one else has the guts to lay down the law so I'm speaking for everyone - and I say no one wants to hear another word from you.

KAREN. When they get long, I'm speaking now of the fingernails, when they get long, they are intolerable. When they get long, they tear and puncture my face. The toenails are worse, they begin to cannibalize the toes inside my shoe.

PHIL. You are dangerous, no one knows where you are coming from - I mean, you confuse people.

SPENCER. I'm not hurting anyone.

PHIL. You're scaring people.

SPENCER. People pay to see horror films. They pay hundreds and hundreds of dollars.

KAREN. And my skin keeps flaking off. I can't tell you how many times I've run the nails across my skin and gotten a full harvest jammed between the finger and the nail. It's disgusting.

AYUN. We make all kinds of crazy transitions.

GREG A. You are wrong.

ADRIAN. We are always the same.

HEATHER. Yeah, shut up.

KAREN. I keep trying to lengthen the intervals between cuttings by cutting them as close as possible to the part that's stuck to the skin, but the shorter I cut them, the faster they grow.

DAVE. I don't believe in God.

TED. Then what do you believe in?

DAVE. I don't know man, but I don't believe in any of the gods I've heard about.

TED. If I were you I'd keep quiet about that, man, just keep it to yourself - I mean if you expect to get that money from the National Endowment.

KAREN. And then there's the hair...not just on the head but everywhere - I just can't pull it out fast enough.

CURTAIN

CHOICE OF VEGETABLE
©1991 by Tim Reinhard

(The play opens with Ted taking orders waiter-style from the cast members who are seated on stage as if around a single table.)

TED. Hi, my name is Ted, are you all ready to order?

TIM. Yes, I'll start. I'll have the nasty divorce with huge alimony payments, the type A personality with huge ulcers, a happy childhood, and could you make sure that's really happy?

TED. Sure.

TIM. Great. And a healthy dose of optimism.

TED. Would you like a sense of fashion with that?

TIM. Maybe later. *(Tim hands Ted his menu.)*

TED. Very good, and for you sir?

PHIL. Yeah, gimme the bitchy ex-wife, a big screen t.v., some, uh, some street smarts, lots of those, and what's this, uh, glimmer of hope for the future? How much is that? Oh, what the hell, gimme that. And a dominating, chauvinistic husband for the little lady here. That should do it for me. *(Phil takes Spencer's menu, who is seated to his left, and hands it to Ted along with his own.)*

BETSY. How's the psychology degree?

TED. It's not great.

BETSY. Not great, huh? You know what, I'm going to have it anyway. And a vacation home in Florida, and I'd really like some intolerant conservative in-laws. Does anyone else want some of those? *(All express interest.)*

TED. They actually come by the bucketful. Shall I bring a whole bucket?

BETSY. That's perfect. And what else, I too will have the happy childhood, that sounds good, and...a son.

TED. One?

BETSY. One, on drugs. And I will have a sense of fashion. *(Betsy hands Ted her menu)*

TED. Great. I think you're going to enjoy that.

GREG K. I have a question...the heterosexual lifestyle...how is that?

TED. *(Slight pause)* It's, uhm, it's not for everyone.

GREG K. Doesn't sound like you recommend it.

TED. Well, actually, I've never tried it. We do have a bisexual combo platter it you want to try a number of different things.

GREG K. Okay...you know what, I'm going to have the passive aggressive personality, with emotional unavailability. And I'll have a heart attack. *(Greg K. hands Ted his menu.)*

AYUN. I know exactly what I want. I'll have the left-wing, anti-capitalist, bohemian lifestyle. Homeschooling for the children. Wild, liberated sexuality. And a mastectomy. But I'll have that later. *(Ayun hands Ted her menu.)*

GREG K. You know what, I'll have my heart attack with her mastectomy.

GREG A. I have a question about the pompous, well-meaning, misguided identity. Is that loud as well?

TED. Yes, it is.

GREG A. And self-righteous?

TED. Somewhat.

GREG A. Okay, good, I'll take that. And an unhappy childhood. Could you make sure that it's really unhappy?

TED. Sure. And would you like a sense of fashion with that?

GREG A. No, I'm fine as I am. *(Allen hands Ted his menu.)*

TED. Uh huh... Okay, I'll be out in a minute with bread and water.

GREG K. *(Clearing his throat, bows head, everyone joins him.)* Bless us, O Lord, for these gifts we are about to receive. That they may nurture us and help us to grow ever closer to our true nature. Amen.

ALL. Amen.

CURTAIN.

<u>CHOP OFF MY HEAD AND 2 GROW BACK</u>
©1992 by Dave Awl

(Dave sits downstage center with his back to the audience. Ayun sits upstage extreme right and Heather upstage extreme left, facing the audience, so that the three form a triangle. Heather's lines are spoken about halfway into Ayun's, so that their dialogue overlaps; the two women seem unaware of each other's presence.)

AYUN. What would you like to talk about?
HEATHER. How have you been?
DAVE. I don't know. I think I'm okay.
AYUN. You seem a little confused.
HEATHER. You seem kind of down.
DAVE. I guess I'm just a little stressed.
AYUN. Can you talk about it?
HEATHER. Is it something you can describe?
DAVE. I think I'm being impersonated. I think someone else is posing as me.
AYUN. Who's impersonating you?
HEATHER. Do you know who it is?
DAVE. It's me. I mean, I'm not the original me. I'm just this...replica.
AYUN. Tell me about it.
HEATHER. Can you talk about it?
AYUN. I mean, how did you find this out?
HEATHER. How did you discover this?
DAVE. I woke up one morning and I found that I had been replaced with a sort of scale model of myself. The copy was perfect in every detail except that it seemed to lack strong emotions about any of things which had previously been important to me.
AYUN. Did you dream this?
HEATHER. Is this real or something you imagined?
AYUN. Maybe that's not important.
HEATHER. How do you think this happened?
DAVE. There was this...salesman who let me take the new me out for some kind of test drive. He told me it was superior to the original in both performance and design. I told him it handled like a dream but I felt a little like New Coke.
AYUN. About your emotions...
HEATHER. You say this new version of yourself didn't have any strong feelings.
AYUN. Did you test this out?
HEATHER. How did you become aware of this?
DAVE. The usual things. Lack of enthusiasm. Can't write anything. Indifference to Beatles songs.
AYUN. So how did this happen?
HEATHER. Who do you think is responsible?
DAVE. Well, my friend Corby thinks it has to do with crop circles in England and the grey aliens. Another friend of mine thinks the CIA is behind it. But I think I sold myself for some quick emergency cash.
AYUN. So what do you do now?
HEATHER. Where do we go from here?

DAVE. Well, there's one major question: how much am I willing to pay to get myself back?
AYUN. That seems logical.
HEATHER. That sounds like a good stopping place for this week.
AYUN. You've raised some good issues.
HEATHER. I think you're making real progress.
AYUN. Same time next week?
HEATHER. Should we make it the usual time?
DAVE. Sure, I'll see you guys then.
AYUN. What?
HEATHER. Excuse me?

CURTAIN

A CHORUS LINE

©1990 by Spencer Kayden

(Cast stands in "V" formation a la "Chorus Line," left hand on imaginary hat brim, right hand on hip, right leg extended. The first four measures of song "ONE" are heard — the cast prepares to start, but the same measures keep repeating themselves, over and over and over again. After five repetitions, the music fades...)

VOICE OVER. What would you do if you could never dance again?

(The music comes back in, still repeating. The song never starts. The cast is horror stricken.)

CURTAIN

CLOWN
©1990 by Lisa Buscani

(33 men are pre-selected from the audience. At the beginning of the piece, they are asked to come up and lie down on the stage. Lisa stands amid them.)

LISA.
My boy
fly boy
Sky
stood on the platform
and waited for the train.
In the season of time
at the time of night
when the fetid air
and lack of light
remind you that
the world is cold
and you are alone.

But he was not.
The man slicked his hair back like
fake teddy boy glory,
wore a grin as sticky
as greasepaint,
groomed his full black moustache,
the talisman of butch prowess,
cinched his ever-expanding waistline
in a bloated line of power,
and kept his mind tight.

Had he ever considered the clown?
the man asked Sky
that the right face could be so basic
in any occupation.
that laughter hitches in the throat with no notice,
the simple, delightful element
of surprise. . .
Clown faces ran from the man's paint brush often
and would Sky like to see?
The man thrust a sunny hand forward,
drew up a big-sky stance,
opened his smile wide
and introduced himself as
John Wayne Gacy.

Sky stepped back.
Stepped back from possible futures,
sidestepped to the ready shell kept
for friendly strangers,

stepped apart from the boys
who wore their blood in their pout,
who could reconcile a moment of sex
with a lifetime of survival,
who had tasted just enough bad days
to pan hope from the attentions
of a sad, fat, old queen,
whose throats circled small
in the onset of horror,
whose lips parted with
the force of constricted wind,
whose screams raced under
and above their skin,
whose eyes were flat
as the beat they lost.
Thirty-three boys,
wrapped in shadow
thirty-three boys,
bathed in freeze frame,
thirty-three boys,
lying soft in their blood.

Sky stepped back.
No, man
no.

CURTAIN

COUNTING
©1989 by Lisa Buscani

(Lisa stands before the audience.)

LISA. My mother is very direct. That's why we're friends.
Once, while drunk on maternal recognition of my maturity, I slipped on a casual reference to some collegiate bed-hopping I'd done. I figured, hell, she was just Catholic, she wasn't dead.
I expected some kind of motherly admonishment because she's into that, but she just looked at me. And then she said:
"Lisa, I spent two weeks watching your uncle die of AIDS. We got there at the very end when he was at his very worst. Once, I remember a nurse put a breathing tube down his throat, and she said, "Does it hurt? Are WE in pain?" And he shook his head no. But when I asked him, I said: "John, are you okay? Does it hurt?" He shook his head yes and closed his eyes and went with it, because that's all that any of us could do, really.
And when it looked like he was going to be on a respirator permanently, we got together as a family and we gave him two weeks and sat there in that hospital room and I said:
John
You've got two weeks left, honey, you better pull out of it . . .
John
You've got eight days left . . .
six days . . .
four days . . .
You've got two days left, John . . .
Until we had to let him go.
And frankly, Lisa, I don't think that a little piece of latex is too much to ask for the sake of your body and your mother's piece of mind."
My mother's direct, boy. That's why we're friends.

CURTAIN

DANDELION WINE
©1989 by Karen Christopher

KAREN. I called my father —

MELISSA. Hi Dad it's me.

KAREN. — And he said:

ROBIN. Ashes to ashes, a regular daffodil.

Whenever the sun doesn't shine I tip over a little.

You want me to call you back what's your number?

KAREN. I gave him my number —

MELISSA. 286-9868

KAREN. — And he said:

ROBIN. That looks really sexy, don't you know. Look at all those sixes and those eights.

KAREN. I said —

MELISSA. How are you?

KAREN. — And he said:

ROBIN. There's not enough in a computer.

Now she's a big adult, big legs, dirty looks.

And the foot that extends all the way to the medulla.

KAREN. I said —

MELISSA. Why don't you call me back later?

KAREN. — and he said:

ROBIN. I'm going to get me some dandelions in a gunny sack and create a little alcohol and come to visit you traveling only at night on my dandelion powered unicycle.

Travail; northern lights so brilliant but so jagged that you don't know where it begins and you think it's going to end.

CURTAIN

DEJA VU
©1989 by Greg Allen

(When the title "Deja Vu" is announced the entire ensemble attempts to repeat the exact action from the previous play as precisely as possible. This includes the set up, the "GO!", the tossing of the paper wad, and any audience interaction, fuck-ups, or mis-cues. The curtain is called after the entire previous play is repeated.)

CURTAIN

DO WHAT YOU WILL
©1992 by Scott Hermes

(Phil comes out and sets a timer. If and when the timer goes off or finishes, Phil will say: "The time to do what you will has passed. Please return to your seats. Process information passively without regard to its validity. Accept all judgments as your own.")

PHIL. For the next 2 minutes and thirty seconds you are free to do as you please. You may get up and move about freely. You may come down and talk to the actors. You may leave the room. You may listen to what I am saying. You may talk to your neighbor and not share it with anyone. You may write below this line.

HEATHER. For the next 2 minutes and 15 seconds you are bound by codes of conduct as old as society itself. You may not get naked. You may not commit incest. You may not pass GO without collecting $200. You may not be able to re-enter the theater without having to pay admission.

GREG K. For the next 2 minutes we, the actors, are locked into a pre-ordained pattern of behavior. We may not deviate from the script. We may not leave the room. We may not finish our *(leaves the room.)*

AYUN. For the next 1 minute and 45 seconds you will do more or less what you have done all your life. Some of you will act without thinking. Some of you will wait until you have figured out what this play is about before taking any action, lest you be thought the fool. Some of you will watch others, to take your cue from them. Some of you will be waiting for me to describe the feelings that you are experiencing right now in the misguided hope that you are really not the only one who could think such thoughts.

SCOTT. For the next 1 minute you will seize this opportunity to surprise yourself. You will act in a way contrary to your own expectations. You will discover a sense of freedom that will stay with you for the rest of your life.

GREG K. *(From next room)* The play has moved into this room. All of you people who stayed in that room are missing the play. Here is where the true meaning lies. All that is in that room are lies and deceptions.

HEATHER. *(Closing door)* The play is in here.

(Greg continues, improvising about free will, and walking around to the other side of the theater.)

HEATHER. *(cont.)* Plays have always taken place on stages surrounded by audiences. In this manner individual experience is transcended and a catharsis is reached. To watch such things alone is no more than voyeurism, and punishable to the full extent of the law.

PHIL. For the next 45 seconds you may do what you want.

AYUN. You cannot do what you want without doing what we want. Our wills are joined. You cannot make a decision now that has not already received our tacit approval, even if that decision is not to decide anything at all.

GREG K. *(Offstage left)* Here is where the play is. Here is where the play is. Plenty of significance and signifiers over here.

SCOTT. For the next 15 seconds -

PHIL. You may -

HEATHER. You may not -

AYUN. Whatever you think is OK with me.

GREG K. This play is over.

SCOTT. For the next -
PHIL. You may-
HEATHER. - or may not -
AYUN. - do
GREG K. This play stopped a long time ago.
SCOTT. For the next time in your life when someone says, "What do you want to do?" or "Would you rather stay in or go out?" and you reply "Whatever you what do is fine by me."

CURTAIN

DON'T LOOK DOWN
©1990 by Dave Awl

(Dave stands on a chair which has been placed center stage. A second chair has been placed immediately stage right of the one Dave stands on.)

DAVE. I wanted to write a play which would be entirely about falling. About people's primal fear of falling, and how so many of the sudden and surprising events in our lives can be compared to taking a nasty spill.

(Dave crosses to the chair to his right, after which Ted surreptitiously moves the chair Dave was just standing on a little further stage left, widening the gap.)

How some people — like for instance myself — feel like we've spent our whole lives falling: plummeting straight down through space without any control over ourselves or where we were headed. I see these people on the street all the time. And wherever I see them, I always recognize them because their hair is standing straight up.

(Between the words "standing" and "straight up" Dave crosses back to the original chair with a single step.)

Sometimes, as we pass, we flail our limbs wildly in a kind of gesture of recognition.

(He demonstrates.)

Other people spend their lives waiting to fall. You recognize these people because they startle easily...

(Dave crosses right to the second chair with a single step, after which Ted moves the chair Dave was just standing on a little bit further to the right, making it impossible for Dave to return. Ted exits.)

...and if you ask them to climb up on a ladder they run for the hills.

(Dave looks at other chair, realizes he can't make it, rolls his eyes and continues.)

I would stage this play in a very special theatre built on top of a deep hole dug thousands and thousands of miles into the earth. There would be a pair of mechanical trap doors underneath the theatre, and at a crucial point in the play the lights would go out.

(Lights go to black.)

And I would pull a giant lever causing the mechanical trap doors to open and the theatre would begin to fall straight down.

(A fan pointing toward the audience is turned on.)

There would be special windows all around the theatre so that we could see the walls of the earth rushing by as we fell.

At first, everyone would be screaming very loudly — but then, after about fifteen minutes or so — there would be absolute silence, except for a sort of thin whistling...

(The other cast members, one by one, begin to whistle softly.)

...which would be the sound of the theatre falling through space. We would sit in the darkness, hypnotized, immobile; entranced by the sound of our own falling, which for the first time in our lives we would be able to hear, clearly. And then, one by one, the other people in the theatre would begin to whistle themselves — their small whistles joining in with the larger whistle, the sound of us all falling... together.

CURTAIN

DUE TUTTA SOLE
©1989 by Karen Christopher

(Karen and Greg Allen are in chairs that are set with their backs on the floor. They are facing the ceiling. Their heads point toward the audience. Their hands are placed on a table between them, also on its side.)

KAREN. I washed my face, I feel better now.

GREG. An isosceles triangle is a triangle that has two equal sides.

KAREN. But I can't rely on water perhaps tomorrow we shall have none.

GREG. If two points are each equidistant from the end points of a segment, then the line joining those two points is the perpendicular bisector of that segment.

KAREN. I don't need water. My needs have become less and less. I may cry but in my crying I am living and this is just another part of my life.

GREG. All objects that make up the universe are separated by unimaginable amounts of almost completely empty space.

KAREN. Did you get a job?

GREG. No. Did you have children?

KAREN. No. *(Pause)* Quarter past four and it's already dark.

GREG. A little colder and it might snow.

CURTAIN

DUELING BIGOTS
©1991 by Betsy Freytag

(Betsy and Spencer are seated in chairs. "Dueling Banjos" plays throughout the play. The following lines are not spoken but delivered with flash cards they hold on their laps. Betsy and Spencer do a slow look to each other.)

BETSY. Snob.
SPENCER. Dumb blonde.
(Tim enters from backstage and crosses between Betsy and Spencer to exit downstage left. Spencer watches Tim intently.)
BETSY. Slut.
SPENCER. Prude.
BETSY. Dyke.
SPENCER. Herpes.
(Greg Allen and Ted cross across the stage from audience left to audience right. Betsy watches them intently.)
SPENCER. Faghag.
BETSY. Homophobe. *(New card)* Midget.
SPENCER. Amazon. *(New card)* Kraut.
BETSY. Jap.
SPENCER. What do you want to bet *(New card)* Her daddy *(New card)* Bought her that car.
BETSY. She probably left *(New card)* Her Tolstoy *(New card)* At the rehab clinic.
SPENCER. Brownnoser.
BETSY. K-Mart.
SPENCER. Jenny Craig Wannabe.
BETSY. Beaneater.
SPENCER. Coke addict.
BETSY. Hippie.
SPENCER. Nazi.
BETSY. Bleeding heart liberal.
SPENCER. Nice dye job.
BETSY. Nice nose job.
(The last two cards are flashed repeatedly.)

CURTAIN

80 IRVING PK RD
©1992 by Dave Awl

(Dave sits center stage. He addresses the audience.)

DAVE. It's a half hour before the pride parade and I'm on the Irving Park Road bus heading east. Sitting in the seats next to me are two petite older women in pantsuits and plastic beads, sunhats and rose-tinted eyeglasses. They're having a loud and impatient discussion of how on earth they're possibly going to find a way to get downtown through the snarled Sunday afternoon traffic. Of course, in the absence of real solutions, this quickly turns into an investigation of the reasons for the crowding. There are repeated references to "the ballgame" and parking patterns, all taken at face value.

And then Edna turns to Agnes and says "and then there's the — the — the *gay* parade." I figure since it took her three *the*'s to get the word gay out, she's obviously not too comfortable with the subject.

This suspicion is confirmed by Agnes who immediately repeats the statement with just a light buttering of incredulous scorn. "The gay parade? What are they parading for...rights?" Edna doesn't quite roll her eyes, but she gives the impression that she would if it were worth the effort. "They're just...parading," she says.

They consider this in irritable silence, then begin discussing possible transportation routes downtown. But as Agnes gets more and more agitated, the question keeps coming back: "*Why* are they parading?" And then Agnes delivers the topper line, the coup-de-grace: "You and *I* don't have a parade."

Now at this point the activist in me is just about ready to jump in and issue the two a brutal corrective, but as usual at times like this, I'm just so overwhelmed by the possible tacks to take that I don't know where to start.

My first thought is the angry one — "You don't have a parade because people like you aren't beaten and killed every day just for being different. You don't have to watch your friends die of AIDS and then see someone on TV say they deserved it for daring to love another person."

The next impulse is the logical, reason-with-them approach: "Of course you have a parade. Every other parade of the year affirms heterosexual culture, from St. Patrick's Day to New Year's — this is the one parade of the year where gay and lesbian people are free to be themselves."

And then comes the third response — the bitchy one. "Well, why don't you start one? I mean you *should* have a parade! Something like, 'Pantsuit Pride!' I can see thousands of cranky women with Marshall Fields shopping bags and sensible shoes proudly high-stepping down Michigan Avenue. 'You look great Agnes!' 'Hold up your head Edna and show your pride, 'cause this is your day!'

Of course I realize that by the time you've degenerated into sarcasm you're not really on the road to positive solutions anymore. And as I watch the two make their brittle way from the bus, I realize that if it's impossible to really educate or inform them during a bus ride, then — while I'm not proud of it — part of me is satisfied to at least see them really inconvenienced.

CURTAIN

FATE DATES THE WEATHERMAN
©1990 by Dave Awl

(Dave and Ted sit onstage.)

DAVE. First something bad happens, and I think, Oh God, life really sucks, every time I turn around something awful happens, I just know something else bad is gonna happen any minute.

TED. And then something good happens, and I think, see, life's not so bad, you just need to relax, good things happen all the time, I just can't wait for the next good thing.

DAVE. And then something bad happens and I think, Oh God, why was I fooled, I'm going downhill fast.

BOTH. And then all of a sudden something good happens.

DAVE. And I think, hey, I'm on the upswing, the bad stuff is behind me, I think big success is just around the corner.

TED. And then something bad happens, and I think this is it, this is the long nose-dive to the ground that I'll never pull out of, my life is over, it's starting now.

DAVE. And then something good happens and I think, you see, why do you waste your life feeling gloomy and wallowing in depression, happiness is all around you if you just look for it!

BOTH. And then something bad happens.

DAVE. And I think, you sickening little fool, how could you be so blind, you're trapped in a long slide toward ruin, caught in a web, the more you struggle the more it's gonna hurt.

TED. And then something wonderful happens, and I think, why are you always such a pessimist, life's too short to spend it on a bummer, these are the best days of your life, I'm gonna climb that mountain and taste the sunshine and live in that gosh darned rose garden!

DAVE. And then something bad happens and I think, you schmuck.

BOTH. You fell for it again.

CURTAIN

FISH
©1990 by Karen Christopher

(Lights off. Karen stands on chair, middle of stage. Randy and Melissa sitting on floor either side of stage. All have flashlights. Lights move as search lights when mic voice speaks, otherwise they shine on speaker.)

KAREN. I got in the passenger's seat of a meat delivery van and the driver took me and my friend to the B & B we were going to be staying at.

TED. *(Breathy voice on microphone)* OK Ladies and Gentlemen, now my head is floating down the street. It's low to the ground, the tendrils hanging out of the severed base of my neck are dangerously close to the gravel on the pavement. I don't want to get the grease and dirt and debris inside the veins running to my brain. It's times like these I wish I were in a meadow in the country.

RANDY. A thousand points of light...what does that mean?

KAREN. If I'd been in America I never would have accepted a ride from a man delivering meat in an unmarked meat delivery van.

TED. Will the audience now make the sounds of a traffic jam in the city?

MELISSA. I didn't vote in the last election, did you?

KAREN. The driver said he and his wife went to Miami for their honeymoon but they'd witnessed a mugging on their first night and she wouldn't leave the hotel for the rest of the week they were there. Therefore he didn't believe he could say he'd actually been to America.

TED. Ladies and Gentlemen, my head is still traveling down the road. Ladies and gentlemen, I'm still trying to keep it clean.

RANDY. What did it sound like when millions of gallons of oil spilled into the ocean?

TED. Ladies and Gentlemen, let us hear what it sounded like.

KAREN. The driver said his wife had watched too many American TV shows — she was convinced America was a very violent place.

TED. Ladies and Gentlemen, my head is still floating down the streets of the city.

KAREN. He dropped us off at our bed and breakfast, got our suitcases out of the back where they were sitting among bags of meat. He said he'd like to come to America but the closest he thought he'd ever get was the telly.

TED. Ladies and Gentlemen, make the sound of the static on your television when there's no program on.

CURTAIN

FOOL-HEARTY
©1990 by Greg Allen

(Greg sits in a chair on stage next to Heather.)

GREG. I love you.
HEATHER. I don't. *(She exits.)*
GREG. I think that's one of the great fears - to lay it all on the line, to take your raw throbbing pulsing beating heart from your chest, hand it to somebody, and they get out their spiked golf shoes and do a demonic tap dance on it. *(Ted enters and sits next to Greg.)*
GREG. I think you're pretty great.
TED. I don't. *(He exits.)*
GREG. But the thing is - you gotta hang in there, you gotta just forge ahead and take the risk that just because you unconditionally give your heart to an ultimately unknown identity, it doesn't necessarily mean they'll put it in one of those ratcheted iron table vices and slowly crush every ounce of living tissue out of it. *(Spencer enters and sits next to Greg.)*
GREG. It was a nice day today, hunh?
SPENCER. No. *(She exits.)*
GREG. I mean just because a certain pattern may seem to be evidencing itself in a kind of bold, tactilely painful way, doesn't mean it will necessarily continue on into a neverending hell equal to having someone slice open your stomach, rip out your intestines, nail them to a tree, and force you to disembowel yourself by running around it! *(Karen enters and sits next to Greg.)*
GREG. Do you know what time it is?
KAREN. Yes, it's about *(the actual time).*
(Pause as Karen smiles at Greg and Greg smiles at the audience.)
GREG. You know, there's always hope - if you're just persistent and go with what you feel. There's always a future, and you never know what it's gonna be.
GREG. I love you.
(Just as she is about to respond someone calls "CURTAIN!")

FROM LITTLE ACORNS
©1992 by Phil Ridarelli

(All are on stage, except for Dave, who enters carrying books.)

TIM. Shh. Here he comes.

BETSY. Hey, Dave, are those your props for this play?

DAVE. You know they are, Betsy. *(She dumps his books.)*

GREG. Aww, is little baby Davey gonna tell his mommy? *(All chant "little baby Davey.")*

TIM. Hey, I think little baby Davey's gonna cry. *(All chant "Davey's gonna cry." Dave goes for his books, Phil kicks them away.)*

AYUN. Hey, Davey, why don't you carry my books for me?

SPENCER. Oh, Annie, you know little baby Davey doesn't carry girl's books. Little Baby Davey doesn't like girls.

PHIL. You mean little baby Davey is a sissy?

GREG. Little baby Davey is a queer-boy?

TIM. Little baby Davey is a sissy.

(Tim pushes Dave over backwards over Phil who has knelt behind him. All chant "Davey is a sissy.")

PHIL. What's wrong, Davey? The truth hurts? Little Davey is a queer-boy? *(Phil wiggles his ass in front of Dave.)*

PHIL. Is that what you like, Davey? Huh, little queer-boy, little faggot, fuckin' homo!

(Dave tries to get up, Phil pushes him back down and threatens him with a stick. The chanting begins to fade.)

PHIL. You stay down there and take it like a man! I swear to fucking god if I ever see your face around here again I'll beat your fucking head in *(Phil strikes the floor 3 times)* you goddamn faggot! *(Silence.)*

CURTAIN

GEORGE SPELVIN IS ALIVE AND WELL
©1991 by Tim Reinhard

(The theater is dark except for a free moving spotlight which fades up and arcs gradually over and around Tim through the course of the following text.)

TIM. Gradually, very gradually, more and more of his face becomes visible, until at last, it is clear that he is none other than who he appears to be. He is exactly himself. A man, illuminated by a single lamp, speaking into the darkness, he is all the image of an actor, on stage during the climactic soliloquy in which the twisted inner workings of his character are revealed. But for this man there is no character. There is no plot. There is no intention. There is no larger context within which he is to be seen. There is no identity for him to get caught up in. No ego to confuse him. There is no history. No habits. No expectations, and he is pleased by simple things, like unrehearsed gestures, knowing they mean nothing and are merely expressions of his being. He is content in his freedom, for he knows that tomorrow he will once more be cast in the role of the sales clerk, and will once more be asked to play the part of the boyfriend, and the family member. So he holds on for a moment longer, and savors the silence and basks in the joy of being himself...alone in the spotlight.

CURTAIN

GOOD MORNING AMERICA
©1992 by Scott Hermes

(Scott stands before the audience.)

SCOTT. Every morning begins with a bark of fear, radio set to the same goddamn, 'XRT station alarm clock, "You're late!" the others are up and gone, already started on their productive lives, miles run, laps swum, sonnets already written, healthy stools passed, flushed, on their way back to be cleansed from your water, children patted on heads, not yet crammed full of defeat, mouths kissed sloppily, mouths as of yet unfamiliar with the sordid taste of compromise, the water thin porridge of our lives, a meal that is easily fixed, yet hard to swallow, whose chefs are reviled, Neville Chamberlin is spat upon, "Peace in our time," waving that thin piece of paper, as if by rooting, by cheering on his desperate hopes, they will become more real, while those glorious, outnumbered, mule-headed, "10,000 Mexicans ain't gonna defeat us" freedom fighters, that's right Norte Americanos, are worshipped and given their own line of vanity accessories, the Bowie Knife, Davy Crockett's coonskin cap, and Sam Houston's Astros, while Santa Anna, who WON for chrissakes, I mean, HE WON, I thought we were a culture that worshipped winners, but I guess that's only OUR winners, Santa Anna doesn't get diddly, not a lousy island, or a city, or a delicious three layer pastry or a creamy beef dish, not national holiday, or monument, or pithy saying, "You've met your Alamo," or even a goddamn car rental agency, and is that supposed to be a COMPLIMENT, did the men turn to one another, manly tears in their historic, soon to be heroic eyes and say, "Waal, these goddamn beaners are gonna be pissing in our open graves by sundown, but by Jesus, we'll live on in countless advertising campaigns, ensuring good service at reasonable rates," and their memory and spirit must live on you think, as you valiantly struggle against that 10,000 strong Mexican bastard, hora, tempus, time, knowing that every moment of warmly nestled, bugly snuggled, dead to the world sleep is a blow against the inevitability of getting up and going to the job you hate.

CURTAIN

GOODNIGHT, SWEETHEART
©1992 by Phil Ridarelli

(The theatre is illuminated only by a night-lite, perhaps a Mickey Mouse or Bugs Bunny type, a cute clown with balloons. Next to the light Phil is lying on the floor, on his back, under a blanket, his head on a pillow, his hands folded behind his head. His eyes are open. A few moments of silence. We hear heels clicking across the floor. 7 steps, silence. 7 steps, silence. 7 steps, silence. This continues throughout the play. After 3 sets of steps we hear...)

AYUN. Honey, will you check on the baby? I think he's thirsty.
(We hear water being poured back and forth between two pitchers.)
DAVE. Listen, I can't stay. I really should be going.
(Steps and water continue. They are joined by "Moonlight Serenade" playing softly.)
LISA. You're going to be late.
(We hear raindrops.)
DAVE. We'll still see each other, you can come visit me, you'll see, I promise.
(Sounds continue.)
AYUN. Listen, I should be going. I really shouldn't stay.
DAVE. *(Overlapping)* I can't stay. I should be going.
(We hear the sound of a fork clinking the side of a wine glass. All sound ceases.)
GREG K. I had this all worked out, but I guess what I really want to say is that I love you and I wish the best of luck to both of you.
(All sound returns, except for the raindrops. They are replaced by the sound of a deck of cards being shuffled. "Moonlight Serenade" begins to fade out.)
DAVE. And they all lived happily ever after.
(Cards stop being shuffled. Water stops being poured. Final series of 7 steps. A door closes. Phil rolls over.)

CURTAIN

GRASPING THE SITUATION
©1992 by Heather Riordan

(Heather & Greg K. are facing each other, seated. Spencer, Ayun, & Betsy are standing behind Heather.)

GREG K. Do you mind if we don't see each other for awhile?

SPENCER. That's fine—I am so busy with my fabulously successful career.

BETSY. Oh, God, you hate me—I knew this would happen—you're trying to get rid of me.

AYUN. You're seeing someone else—I'm going to poke your eyes out with a sharp stick.

GREG K. It's not that I don't like you...

SPENCER. I know that. I'm a confident 90's woman who listens to subliminal affirmation tapes about how much I like myself.

BETSY. You don't like me at all—I can read it all over your face.

AYUN. You don't appreciate me. I'm going to cut your heart out and eat it raw.

GREG K. It's just that I need some time to focus.

SPENCER. I'm not taking this personally—my self-esteem isn't dependent on other people.

BETSY. I'm a distraction in your life that you're trying to get rid of.

AYUN. You are selfish—you must die.

GREG K. I'm just not sure I'm really ready to be intimate with someone.

SPENCER. I'm so confident about my sexuality I don't even need a partner.

BETSY. Oh, God, you think I'm lousy in bed.

AYUN. You don't appreciate me as a sexual being—I'm going to cut your dick off.

GREG K. So, how're you feeling about all this—are you OK?

HEATHER. Yeah, I just haven't decided what I'm going to do yet.

CURTAIN

HEMINGWAY AFTERNOON
©1990 by Lisa Buscani

(Ted stands center stage with Ayun, Karen, and Melissa standing directly behind him. Ted lights his cigarette.)

TED. We slept, we woke, we ate, we fucked.
(Ted repeats this over and over. Ayun & Melissa step out from behind Ted.)
AYUN & MELISSA. *(simultaneously)* Dahling, I love you. Do you love me?
(Ayun & Melissa also repeat their lines. Randy enters stage left with a beer. He opens it and drinks.)
RANDY. I'm a man. I'm a manly man. The most manly man, I am. *(Randy repeats his line as Karen steps out from behind Ted.)*
KAREN. Closet homosexual. *(Karen repeats her line as Phil and Adrian run towards each other from either side of the stage, leap into the air and yell.)*
PHIL & ADRIAN. Bullfighting!
(And run offstage. All actors repeat their lines until Phil and Adrian repeat "bullfighting" three times. Everyone stops. Lisa enters from stage right.)
LISA. It was good.

CURTAIN

I MAKE MY OWN WEATHER
©1991 by Spencer Kayden

(Spencer stands on stage dripping wet.)

SPENCER. I made it rain yesterday. Pour actually. For no apparent reason. The skies were mostly clear. The weather was unnoticeably perfect. The birds were chirping. Dogs were introducing themselves. The flowers on my street stood at pastel attention. But I couldn't stand it. I turned a 30% chance of rain into a severe late evening thunderstorm. Flash flood warnings stayed in effect until almost midnight. Even when I first noticed it was sprinkling I could have made it stop. But I had my heart set on a torrential downpour complete with bowling alley thunder and lightning that shut the power down. Still I didn't feel soaked enough so I commanded a tremendous hailstorm. And I stood outside in it, convincing myself that the more pelted I am, the more drenched I become, the more coughs I develop, the more pneumonia I contract, then the more deserving I'll be of a warm, dry afternoon.

CURTAIN

I MET A STORM IN OKLAHOMA CITY
©1990 by Karen Christopher

GREG A. Because of the dense fog at O'Hare we are unable to gain clearance. We are forced to remain here on the ground : For an unspecified amount of time : under no circumstances may you leave. Please remain seated as we may receive clearance at a moment's notice.

ADRIAN. Hi.

KAREN. *(To audience)* I met a storm in Oklahoma City.

ADRIAN. I've got to get off this bird, I've got to quit this aircraft, I must deplane.

KAREN. You do what you have to, but they might leave you behind.

ADRIAN. If they did...it would kill me.

KAREN. *(To audience)* I met a storm in Oklahoma City.

ADRIAN. I'm Al, who are you?

KAREN. I'm Karen.

ADRIAN. I've got to talk to someone - I'm going crazy in here...

KAREN. I'm here.

ADRIAN. I'm a Vietnam vet.

KAREN. *(To audience)* No one ever tells you he's a Vietnam vet for no reason.

ADRIAN. I left home a week ago. Went to Las Vegas with nothing but a little money and the clothes on my back. I've had a lousy week — I just need to talk to someone.

KAREN. *(To audience)* Are there any unscarred Vietnam vets?

ADRIAN. It was my birthday last week — I just turned 47. I got drunk I woke up the next day and I didn't have my car keys — I was trapped man, no vehicle, no transport —— I just said — fuck man — I'm GETTING OUT of here, I'VE HAD ENOUGH. I'm going to do something about this.

KAREN. *(To audience)* Did anyone ever come home from a war unscarred?

ADRIAN. My girlfriend took my keys, man, she took them to work with her when I called she said come and get them if you are sober now — what? I said — take the bus?!!! No way! I'm not taking a damn bus man I can't do it! So I just took off for the airport I just said fuck it. I'm in a fucking pressure cooker! I'm going to Las Vegas, now.

KAREN. Hey man it's OK cool it now, hey yeah, take a chill, no one realized you would flip out that way. They didn't know.

ADRIAN. Well I know and it sucks. Hey, I'm getting off this plane. I'm history.

CURTAIN

I REMEMBER THE LEG
©1989 by Dave Awl

(Lisa sits downstage center. Ayun, Dave and Adrian stand on stage with their backs to the audience.)

LISA. Sure, I remember the Leg. You see, I was the Leg's adoptive mother. It happened like this. I was on my way home from doing some shopping, and well, there was the Leg lying in a patch of grass looking kind of stunned. I remember thinking it was strange to see a leg all by itself like that. Well, I went over and started massaging its foot, and pretty soon it started to revive. After another minute or so it was feeling good enough to get to its foot, and well, to make a long story short, it ended up following me home, sort of hopping along behind me. Of course the kids just loved the Leg. Pretty soon, the Leg seemed like one of the family, and it was hard to imagine what life would be like without the Leg.
(Lisa turns upstage. Ayun turns to face the audience.)
AYUN. Of course I remember the Leg! I was the Leg's sister. It was my job to take the Leg to the shoe store to get it a shoe which always presented a problem, of course, because there was only one Leg and it only needed one shoe. The right one. It was a right leg. Shoes get sold in pairs and it just seemed like such an awful waste to buy two shoes for one leg. I remember the first time it happened, I said to the Leg, "Don't you have a match somewhere, you know, someone just like you only opposite?" Well, the Leg didn't like that one bit. It got very perturbed. It flexed its toes angrily. It was then that I sensed that the Leg was capable of great violence somehow. So I just let it go and paid for the pair.
(Ayun turns back to face upstage. Dave turns to face the audience.)
DAVE. I remember the Leg. I remember the Leg because the Leg kicked my ass. Repeatedly. The first time it happened I was just walking down the street, minding my own business, and I stopped to tie my shoe. Out of the corner of my eye, I had noticed the Leg making its way down the other side of the street, but I didn't think anything of it, of course not, I didn't think a thing. Well, as I'm bending over, I glance behind me and what do I see but the Leg, sailing through the air toward my butt. There was no time to duck or try to avoid it. Before I knew what hit me, the Leg had left its footprint on my booty, and I couldn't sit down for days. No — I didn't like that leg one bit.
(Dave turns to face upstage. Adrian faces audience.)
ADRIAN. Yeah, I remember the Leg all right. I'll always remember the Leg. You see, the Leg killed my father. It was an argument over a card game. My father was playing cards with the Leg and some other guys, and the Leg won a hand. It was a straight flush — all clubs. It was then that my father spoke those fateful, tragic, idiotic words: "So, I guess this makes you a club foot." Well, the leg didn't like that at all. And — thank God I wasn't there to see it — but from what I understand, the Leg then stomped on my father 5,280 times — till he was just dead. Yeah, I remember. I'll always remember that fuckin' leg.
(Adrian turns upstage. Lisa turns to face audience.)
LISA. I remember the Leg.
(Ayun turns to face the audience.)
AYUN. I remember the Leg.
(Dave turns to face the audience.)
DAVE. I remember the Leg.
(Adrian turns to face the audience.)
ADRIAN. I remember the fuckin' Leg.

CURTAIN

I WANT YOU
©1991 by Greg Kotis

(Phil & Spencer dance slowly while embracing.)

SPENCER. I want you to love me.
PHIL. I do.
SPENCER. I want you to love those whom I love.
PHIL. I can.
SPENCER. I want you to love me for the love I have.
PHIL. I will.
SPENCER. And I want you to love me.
PHIL. I do.
SPENCER. *(Pause.)* I want you to hate those whom I hate.
PHIL. I don't.
SPENCER. I want you to love me for the hate I have.
PHIL. I don't.
SPENCER. I want you to love the hate we share.
PHIL. I don't.
SPENCER. And I want you to love me.
PHIL. I do.
SPENCER. Say it.
PHIL. *(Pause)* I hate them.
SPENCER. I love you too.

CURTAIN

I'D OFFER YOU SOME, BUT THIS IS MY DINNER
©1991 by Greg Kotis

(Greg and Karen sit on chairs facing the audience. Greg begins unwrapping a sandwich he holds on his lap.)

GREG. There was a fire on the train today. When the train stopped, the conductor left the car I was in to investigate. He was gone several minutes. When he returned a passenger asked him what was wrong. The conductor replied recession in America, taxes were too high, he had to work for a living. Soon after, the train began moving.

KAREN. I heard that on his recent trip to Chicago, the President visited the Billy Goat Tavern to talk to working people about the economy. Of course, he ordered a cheeseburger, chips (no fries), and a Pepsi (no Coke). When the President asked for the check, the proprietor said the meal was on the house, but that he could pay the next time he came. Of course, the President agreed.

(Karen watches as Greg lifts the sandwich he has been holding to his mouth. Greg hesitates, lowers the sandwich, and turns to Karen.)

GREG. Don't look at me like that.

CURTAIN.

I'D RATHER BE JUMPING THE GRAND CANYON
©1991 by Phil Ridarelli

(Greg Allen and Greg Kotis stand stage left. Phil stands center stage wearing a crash helmet. Heather, Tim, and Dave attend to him. Ted and Lisa watch enthusiastically from an upstage riser.)

GREG ALLEN & GREG KOTIS. Hi! I'm Greg and he's Greg!

GREG KOTIS. And we're here live at Live Bait Theatre where the Neo-Futurists are just about to begin another of the 30 plays they'll attempt to perform in 60 minutes.

GREG ALLEN. Yes, Greg, we can just get a glimpse of the Neo-Futurists setting up for this next performance.

GREG KOTIS. So tell me Greg, is this a comedy we'll be seeing? A tragedy, parody, or some personal revelation by one of the Neo-Futurists?

GREG ALLEN. Well, Greg, it's a little bit of each.

GREG KOTIS. Really? Well, my goodness.

GREG ALLEN. Yes, really, Greg. In this play we're going to see Neo-Futurist Phil Ridarelli attempt a truly amazing feat. I've been told it's quite a challenge for him.

GREG KOTIS. Really? Well, my goodness.

GREG ALLEN. Yes, really, Greg. But the beauty of this piece is that this incredible challenge is disguised as some type of cheap Evel Knievel sports stunt spectacular so as to draw any focus away from the real issue.

GREG KOTIS. Which is?

GREG ALLEN. A man who is experiencing a lot of pain and guilt.

GREG KOTIS. Really? Well, my goodness.

GREG ALLEN. Yes, really.

GREG KOTIS. Well, my goodness. I can't imagine what Phil is going to attempt. I mean we've shared his skydiving experience, he's told us of the time he fought three guys twice his size...

GREG ALLEN. And how can anyone forget that drunken pre-dawn ride home from Wisconsin?

GREG KOTIS. I don't think even Phil realized what a risk that was.

GREG ALLEN. Well, Greg, those stunts are simply dwarfed by what Phil is going attempt today.

GREG KOTIS. Why don't we go down to Ayun who is with Phil now. *(Ayun enters and stands beside Phil.)*

AYUN. Greg!

GREG ALLEN & GREG KOTIS. Ayun!

(Greg Allen & Greg Kotis give a slow burn to each other.)

AYUN. I'm here, live, less than five feet away from you speaking as if there is much activity going on around me. Phil has been preparing for what I'm sure is going to be a spectacular feat. Phil, could you share with the folks sitting in front of us what it is you're going to attempt today?

PHIL. Sure, Ayun. I'm going to forgive those who have hurt me and ask forgiveness from those whom I have hurt.

ALL. Ooh. Wow. Oh. My goodness.

AYUN. My goodness, Phil. Of all the challenges you've faced, this one seems to be the most directly tied to your Catholic upbringing.

PHIL. Yes. I'm sorry.

AYUN. We hear you've been training very hard and long to meet this challenge.

PHIL. Yes, I started early last year forgiving people for, uhm, cutting me off in traffic, bumping into me in a crowd, or maybe just stepping on my heel causing it to...God, I hate that.

AYUN. And what about asking for forgiveness?

PHIL. Oh, goodness, Ayun, where do I start?

AYUN. Busy, huh?

PHIL. I'll say.

AYUN. Well, Phil, good luck, we're all with you.

(Ayun smacks Phil's helmet.)

AYUN. Back to you, Greg.

GREG ALLEN & GREG KOTIS. Thanks, Ayun.

(Greg Allen & Greg Kotis give a slow burn to each other.)

GREG ALLEN. Well, it looks as though Phil is ready to give it a shot.

GREG KOTIS. Boy, you can tell this is very difficult for him. Look at the tension in his body. Listen to the way I've started whispering.

GREG ALLEN. Ooh. Oh. Here he goes. This could be it.

(Pause. All eyes on Phil. If there was a snare drum you would hear a drum roll.)

PHIL. I...would like to... I can't...

(Phil collapses. All react as if he's broken both his legs in four places. Tim, Heather, Dave, Ayun rush to Phil.)

GREG ALLEN. Dear Lord, Greg, did you see that?

GREG KOTIS. He went down in a ball of flames!

GREG ALLEN. That had to hurt.

GREG KOTIS. You could see the moment where he holds on to all that guilt.

GREG ALLEN. Yes. Yes. If he could just let it go.

GREG KOTIS. I've never seen a man so devastated, so humiliated, so...so...

GREG ALLEN. Let's see that again!

(All rewind and playback the moment in slo-mo.)

GREG KOTIS. Jesus, it looks even worse the second time around.

GREG ALLEN. That was truly awful. Let's take another look at that!

PHIL, AYUN, DAVE, HEATHER, & TIM. Oh, Jesus, c'mon, give'im a break, for god's sake. Back off, huh? *(Tim, Heather, & Dave support Phil.)*

CURTAIN

THE IDEA OF YOU
©1991 by Dave Awl

(Dave Awl and Phil Ridarelli sit center stage in two chairs with their backs to each other.)

DAVE. I called you up and I said How were you and could I please speak to the Idea of You? You said Excuse me? I said I didn't call to talk to you, I called to talk to the Idea of You. I said I had been doing some thinking. I had realized that all the time I had been seeing you, it was really the idea of you I wanted to go out with. You asked me how I had come to this astonishing conclusion. I said Oh, little things had tipped me off: the way you knocked over your water glass last Wednesday, when the idea of you was grace and ease. The way you fumbled for words on Sunday, but the idea of you always knew what to say. I said I always understood the idea of you, but lately you were beginning to confuse me. *(Phil rises to stand beside his chair.)* There was a momentary pause as you handed over the receiver, and then a voice came on the line that reminded me of you but without those annoying glitches and halts. We talked for a few moments in what felt like a carefree, ideal way; and then the Idea of You asked to speak to the Idea of Me. I asked for clarification of this bizarre suggestion - and it asserted that the Idea of Me was too sensitive and intelligent to reject the human imperfections of someone I loved. *(Pause.)* Sensing that I had somehow dropped the ball, I nobly stepped aside *(Dave rises to stand beside his chair. Both Phil and Dave regard the two empty chairs.)* so that the Idea of Us could live happily ever after.

CURTAIN

INDELIBILITY
©1992 by Heather Riordan

(Greg K. & Heather are center stage, Greg K. standing & Heather sitting in a chair. Greg. A., Phil, & Spencer are leaning against the back wall, at varying heights.)

GREG K. There's a stain on my shirt.
HEATHER. That little spot there, yeah, I tried to get it out.
GREG K. It's a stain.
HEATHER. Yeah, whatever.
GREG K. No, I don't think you appreciate the gravity of the situation.
HEATHER. It's just a small spot—I can hardly see it.
GREG K. Let me explain: it was a spot, just a spot, until you didn't get it out. You just didn't care enough to remove it. Now it's festered and grown into a stain because of your neglect and this shirt is forever tainted.
HEATHER. It's just a small stain.
GREG K. No stain is ever small.
GREG A., PHIL, & SPENCER. *(Singing.)*
There's a stain on your blouse and it won't go away
There's a ring around your collar that shows in the light
There's a dingy tinge of grayness to your once
to your white
to your socks

CURTAIN

IT'S A BREEZE
©1991 by Greg Allen

(Greg Allen, Mike, Robin and Randy stand on stage.)

ALL. Hi.
MIKE. We're male.
GREG. And white.
ROBIN. Not only that, but we're young.
RANDY. Yup, four young white men.
GREG. Think of the power.
MIKE. You know, life's a breeze when you're young, white, and male.
RANDY. Yup, we can do anything we want to.
ROBIN. We can go anywhere we please.
GREG. The future is anything we want to make it.
MIKE. We can be head of the household.
ROBIN. We can run large corporations.
GREG. We can be elected to major political offices.
RANDY. Like mayor.
ROBIN. Or president.
MIKE. All because we're young, white, and male.
GREG. Thank god we're not women.
RANDY. Or black.
ROBIN. Or queer.
GREG. You mean you're not...?
ROBIN. No.
MIKE. *(To Greg)* I thought you were?
GREG. No, not me. *(to Randy)* Maybe...?
RANDY. No, don't look at me.
GREG. Oh my god! And straight! We've got it made!
MIKE. You know, the other day I hired one of us for a job.
(Others congratulate him.)
ROBIN. I just wrote a book about one of us.
(Congrats.)
GREG. You know last night, I went to the theater and saw a play about being just like us.
(High praise from the others.)
RANDY. *(To the others)* Who are you going to vote for in the next election?
OTHERS. *(after looks of confirmation)* One of us.
MIKE. You know, life's a breeze for us. We can do anything we want to...because...
ALL. We're young, we're white, we're straight, and we're male.

CURTAIN
(Followed by massive booing.)

KING LEAR
©1988 by Greg Allen

(Greg Allen is Lear, Randy is Reagan, Rex Jenny is Cordelia, and Robin is the Announcer. Lear sits in a chair center stage wearing a coat and tie. Announcer is upstage.)

ANNOUNCER. "The Tragedy of King Lear" by William Shakespeare. Act One.
(Reagan walks on from stage left to meet Lear and stops.)
LEAR. Do you love me?
REAGAN. Yes.
(Reagan exits stage left. Lear is pleased. Reagan again enters and stops beside Lear.)
LEAR. Do you love me?
REAGAN. Yes.
(Reagan exits. Lear is more pleased. Cordelia enters from stage right to meet Lear and stops.)
LEAR. Do you love me?
CORDELIA. *(Pause.)* Nothing.
(She hangs her head and exits stage right.)
LEAR. What?!
ANNOUNCER. Act Two.
(Lear is blind. He slowly stands up and begins to feel his way around the stage. Reagan walks on from stage left and is stopped by Lear who hears him and grabs him by the shoulders.)
LEAR. Do you love me?
REAGAN. Yes.
(Lear removes his coat and gives it to him. Reagan continues on to exit stage right. Lear gropes around the stage. Reagan, crossing from stage right to left, is again stopped by Lear.)
LEAR. Do you love me?
REAGAN. Yes.
(Lear gives him his shirt and tie. Reagan exits. Reagan enters stage left and is stopped by Lear.)
LEAR. Do you love me?
REAGAN. Yes, yes, yes.
(Lear removes his watch and gives it to him. Reagan begins to exit and thinks better or it. He taps Lear on the shoulder who turns and grabs him.)
LEAR. Do you love me?
REAGAN. You bet.
(Lear removes both of his shoes and gives them to Reagan. Reagan takes them and exits stage right disappointed. Lear is left alone on stage. He hears noises from the audience and walks towards whomever he hears. When he runs into someone, he holds them by the shoulders and asks, "Do you love me?" If they say yes, he gives them his socks. He then moves towards whoever laughs the loudest, finds them, and again asks "Do you love me?" If they say yes, he gives them his pants. He again moves towards the person who laughs the loudest and, holding them by the shoulders, asks "Do you love me?" If they respond yes, he gives them his shorts. He is left alone, blind, and naked on the stage. He backs up, attempts to cover himself, and says "Lear I Nothing Am." If at any time someone responds in the

negative he does the same thing, retaining his remaining clothes. Lear then gropes his way off stage.)
ANNOUNCER. Act Three.
(Cordelia enters from stage left carrying a bag. Reagan meets her center stage and politely seats her in the chair. He then takes her bag and kneels on the floor. He removes a styrofoam head and a saw, and proceeds to saw the head through at the eyes making as much excruciating noise as possible. While he does this Cordelia slowly goes blind. He puts the saw and the two parts of the head back in the bag, returns it to Cordelia, and exits stage left. Cordelia rises and gropes her way off stage right.)
ANNOUNCER. Act Four.
(Lear crawls on from stage left wearing a coat (if he was naked) and Cordelia crawls on from stage right. They crawl towards each other but miss and pass each other. They stop, sensing each other's presence, and crawl back towards each other but miss again. They again stop and crawl towards each other and meet. Lear grabs Cordelia by the shoulders and desperately asks, "Do you love me?" She does not answer for she has gone deaf. Lear continues to shake her and ask "Do you love me?" until Reagan crosses the stage and throws a glass of water in Lear's face. Lear sees that it is Cordelia, clutches her to his chest, and quietly says, "Howl...howl...howl.")

CURTAIN

THE LAST TIME I SAW JANE
©1990 by Ayun Halliday

(Randy, Phil, and Adrian beat a primitive bongo beat on their stomachs. Ayun, Lisa, and Karen stand arms akimbo with their legs spread wide.)

AYUN. The last time I saw Jane she was swinging through the trees, singing.
Me no hang with that big ape, me lose taste for jungle rape!
Me no sad, me feeling fine, me make my own way vine by vine.
I knew it was Jane by the muscles in her back.
(The men yip and howl. The women dance.)
LISA. The last time I saw Jane I saw her from the inside.
It was a Tuesday in December and she's eaten me up
With some five-alarm chili and a half a box of oyster crackers.
She was a powerful woman, that Jane.
I enjoyed the few hours that I spent inside her,
Snug and warm on that wintry afternoon.
(The men yip and howl. The women dance.)
KAREN. The last time I saw Jane she was wearing a frock of live snakes.
I said, "Jane, it's gorgeous, but what if they bite?"
Jane just gave me that look of hers and rearranged some coils
To expose her tattoo.
Venom was a luxury she could afford.
"Jane, it's stunning," I said.
And it was.
(The men yip and howl once more, the women dance out of control, ending on an abrupt beat.)

CURTAIN

LINEAR PROGRESS
©1992 by Greg Kotis

(Greg Kotis speaks while flying superman-style, balancing himself parallel to the floor on a podium.)

GREG. I had this dream where I was flying. I was very high up. So high, in fact, that I was just able to touch the top of the Sear's Tower antenna as I passed over downtown Chicago. *(Dave Awl crosses past Greg holding a mock-up of the top of the Sear's Tower antenna to simulate the event.)* Of course, I enjoyed this immensely. I mean what could compare to the sensation of flying, entirely unencumbered, and powered entirely by the will to fly. I was flying in a straight line, heading due South. And, in truth, aside from discerning whether or not I was fully clothed, something I was unable to discern...for some reason, this linear progression troubled me more than anything else. I began to worry whether flying straight ahead was any way for a truly inspired flier to fly. Superman was capable of great twists and turns or just hovering if he wanted to. Dog fights were consistently engaging because of the athletic loops and banks the fighter pilots demanded of their aircraft. But there I was flying straight ahead, content to watch Illinois become Indiana and Indiana become...more Indiana. It was at this point that I noticed I wasn't alone. *(Phil, Ayun, and Heather enter and adopt Greg's pose with the help of a chair, a stool, etc., which they've brought on with them.)* In fact the sky was filled with conflicted fliers. Well, maybe they weren't conflicted. I think I just assumed that they were since we were all flying in the same direction. Actually, the guy closest to me seemed reasonably conflicted so I asked him "Does it bother you that given the amazing possibilities of uninhibited flight the best we seem to have come up with is reaching the Gulf of Mexico as soon as possible?" To which he replied...
PHIL. What makes you think it's uninhibited?.
GREG. There was an uncomfortable silence for a few moments, until finally he added to his initial statement...
PHIL. And put some clothes on!
GREG. Everyone seemed thoroughly relieved that some one had mentioned this. And then we all started singing that part from the "Ride of the Valkyries."
ALL. Bah bah bah bah BAH bah, bah bah bah bah BAH bah, bah bah bah bah BAH bah, bah bah bah bah bahhhh...

CURTAIN

LIP READERS
©1990 by Greg Allen

(Before the show begins, three audience members are enlisted to participate. They are each handed a card with a prepared question on it and told to stand and read the question when they are referred to by name during the show. Their names and occupations are written down and given to Phil for the play. At the "Go," Greg Allen and Spencer stand behind podiums. Phil addresses the audience.)

PHIL. Hello my name is Phillip Ridarelli. I'm your moderator this evening for the first of a series of debates between these two candidates who seem to be running for some high political office of some sort. We'll open with a question from *(audience member's name)* who is *(audience member's occupation)*.

FIRST AUDIENCE QUESTIONER. I would like to know where each of the candidates stands on the abortion issue and how you personally and politically justify your position?

PHIL. Greg will respond first.

GREG. Well despite what my opponent may think, I am now and have always been a strong advocate of a woman's right to choose. In my mind it ultimately comes down to the question of who has the right to make this sort of decision. I believe it is the personal choice of the individual and not one that can be made by the government. Thank you.

PHIL. And now Spencer.

SPENCER. Well first I would like to remind my opponent that just because I am a woman, it does not in any way mean that I would assume all men to be against a woman's right to choose. This, I think, is quite a sexist assumption, and might lead one to question why he supposedly upholds these sentiments in the first place. But to answer the question, I am pro-choice right down the line.

PHIL. All right. Now we'll have a question from *(audience member's name)* who is a *(audience member's occupation)*.

SECOND AUDIENCE QUESTIONER. The national deficit is now over three trillion, two hundred and twenty four billion dollars. Do you feel there is really any way to balance the budget without raising taxes astronomically?

PHIL. Greg?

GREG. Well first I would like to respond to my opponent's empty charges of sexism. This is exactly the kind of low petty immoral attack she has used throughout her career in order to avoid important issues. This is not a question of who is the male candidate and who is the female; it is a question of who is honest and trustworthy, and who is the scurvy little backbiting snake. Thank you.

PHIL. Spencer, your response.

SPENCER. First, might I point out that my opponent did not even address the question but has once again turned a dignified intellectual debate into a forum for his own adolescent mudslinging, full of lies and slander. But then, what do you expect from someone who fondles young boys for pleasure. In response to your question: Yes.

PHIL. Okay, next we have a question from *(audience member's name)* who is a *(audience member's occupation)*.

THIRD AUDIENCE QUESTIONER. Do you believe in a national health care plan, and if not, how do you intend to make health care equally accessible to all Americans?

PHIL. Greg, would you like to address this extremely pertinent question?

GREG. First I would just like to remind my opponent that if both of her legs were chopped off at the waist, she would leave a trail of slime on the ground like a snail. Thank you.

PHIL. Spencer?

SPENCER. Does the word "dickless" mean anything to you?

PHIL. Well! I think that concludes the first section of our debates. On to the second round. Best three out of five falls.

(Greg and Spencer get down on their knees in wrestling position and Phil blows a whistle. They avidly wrestle until either Greg absolutely creams Spencer in about two seconds, or he generously allows her believe that she could possible even move his stone-chiseled form to the ground.)

CURTAIN

LITTLE FLIERS
©1991 by Greg Kotis

(The theater is dark except for a spotlight which reveals Greg Kotis standing center stage. As he speaks, the ensemble creates the sound of mosquitoes, gradually building throughout the piece.)

GREG K. Sure, I'm afraid of mosquitoes. Some people aren't. I am. I'm afraid of mosquitoes because they carry disease. And they carry disease because of how they live. They spend their pupal stage, their youth, floating just below the surface of any stagnant, fresh body of water. Of course, they're impossible to see at this stage, impossible to detect. But if your water's stagnant chances are they're there. Just floating beneath the surface. Bloated, invisible, ineffectual mosquito children. But once grown, the adult mosquito emerges from its dormancy to fly through the skies, to seek out the warm-blooded creatures like me, like you, and to feed. Of course the adult mosquito looks as vulnerable as it did as a child. But it's not. And it's not because when it's grown it has the disease. And as an adult it can give it to you. It'll pierce your skin and find your blood, drink until its belly is full and fat, and spit into the vacancy it just created. And when it does that, then you've got the disease. And then you're dead. And in the moments before dying try telling somebody that you're innocent, that you didn't do anything, that you're only guilty of letting them live long enough to kill you. See what they say. So yes, sure, I'm afraid of mosquitoes. And so should you be.

CURTAIN

A LITTLE OFF THE TOP
©1992 by Phil Ridarelli

(Phil is seated with a towel around his neck. Ayun is cutting his hair. They are lit by a spotlight. On the back wall are two slide projections. One of Phil's mom, the other of a Victoria's Secret model.)

PHIL. When I was little my mom would cut my hair. One time she did such a poor job, I hid, crying, in the bathroom for three hours. Then, when I was in high school, my sister went to beauty school and she would practice by cutting everyone in the family's hair. All the Ridarelli's looked identical. Parted down the middle, sides feathered back. Even my dad. And he was bald. I still don't know how she did that. Now I go to a guy on Clark named George. I pay eight dollars for a trim. He plays '40s music in his shop. At this point, you may think this play is about my losing my hair. It's not. I read in the paper last week that a men's hair salon called the Mane Event. M-A-N-E. Just opened across from the Merc. All the hair dressers there are women. They wear nothing but lingerie. If my mom had cut my hair like that I may never have come out of the bathroom. Or my sister for that matter. I guess scantily clad hairdressers doesn't surprise me so much. There's a service that offers housecleaning by women in their underwear. There's a restaurant across the street from where I work that has a lingerie show during the lunch hour. The same woman who filled my coffee cup that morning is slinging hash in crotchless panties at noon. Yes, I'd like a BLT&A. Sometimes these plays just write themselves.
AYUN. Is there anything else, sir?
PHIL. Yes, can you take a little off the top, please?
(She steps in front of him, facing him, and begins to take off her shirt. He gets up, puts his towel around her.)
PHIL. Stop. This is degrading to both of us.

CURTAIN

LOOK, REACH, PULL
©1989 by Phil Ridarelli

(Three chairs sit on stage in a diagonal line facing stage left. Phil addresses the audience.)

PHIL. Have you ever been skydiving? I have. I went with two of my best friends.
AYUN & KAREN. *(Simultaneously)* That was fucking incredible! Did you fucking see it from up there! I couldn't believe you did it! I know! I thought my chute ripped open! Too fucking much!
PHIL. We went to a place in Sandwich, Illinois, called Skydive Sandwich. Yes, really. Someone who once saw this play told me that it's closed now. All the signs keep pointing to the airport but when we got there we found a little country house with a garage out back surrounded by these tiny airplanes with engines about the size of snowblowers.
KAREN. *(To Ayun)* Listen, you jump first so if I fuck up you can catch me.
PHIL. The entire day costs $125. $25 for the equipment rental and $100 for the lessons, which consisted of 5 hours of videotape and 1 hour of practical training.
AYUN. *(To Karen, whispering)* In 3 hours we're going to be jumping out of an airplane.
(Karen experiences a sudden, but intense, fit of the willies.)
PHIL. Dave had already been skydiving so we stayed up the night before so he could teach us the steps in our kitchen. O.K. So, first of all you're wearing this chute on your back which is strapped with a harness and it's real tight. And they have all of you get in this Cessna which is about the size of a Volkswagen so there's 5 of you in this thing, the 3 of you who are jumping, the pilot, who's next to you, and the jump-master, who sits facing you by the door. So you're facing backwards. Then they start taxiing down the runway and everything starts shaking and then all of a sudden the ground falls away from you and you're climbing through the air. Then when you're high enough the jump-master kicks the door open and everything gets very loud! And very cold! And the door keeps swinging and hitting the underside of the wing. Now you have to put a foot on the little step outside of the plane and turn and grab the strut that's attaching the wing to the plane. When you have both hands on the strut you begin to inch your way out of the plane all the time keeping your eyes on the jump-master so you can't tell how fast you're going or how high you are or what a stupid fucking thing you're about to do! Then when you're far enough out when you can reach the little hand-prints they've painted there for you, you actually step off the step so you're dangling there in the air. Then when the jump-master points at you, you look up and there are this little yellow smiley face staring back at you and when you see it you say DOT! GO! and you let go of the airplane and immediately start trying to climb the air back into the fucking plane like some kind of goddamn Bugs Bunny cartoon character and the plane just falls away from you and becomes this little speck in the air. As you fall you say 1 thousand, 2 thousand, 3 thousand, 4 thousand, 5 thousand, LOOK! REACH! PULL!
AYUN & KAREN. DOT! GO! 1000 2000 3000 4000 5000 LOOK! REACH! PULL!
PHIL. And your chute opens and it's silent. All you hear is the wind rushing by you. *(Remaining ensemble members create the sound of the wind.)*
You check your chute. Yep. There it is. You look. Horizon. All around you. There's the earth. Below your feet. 3000 feet below your feet. But it feels so secure. So

safe. You could stay here forever. You check your brakes. Pull the left one, you turn left. The right one, right. If you pull both at the same time your chute stops in midair and you begin falling backwards and that's the scariest fucking thing in the world. Then they have this receiver hooked to your arm and when you get about tree level they tell you to begin braking. And you say Flare, Flare, Flare, and you touch the ground as gently as if you had stepped off a stool.
AYUN & KAREN. Flare, Flare, Flare.
PHIL. Then you gather up your chute and run to the others and say That was fucking incredible! *(Ayun & Karen join him.)* Did you see it from up there! Too fucking much! *(etc.)*
(beat)
KAREN. Then it's time to pay.
AYUN. $125 for a few glorious moments.
KAREN. Then it's time to head back home.
AYUN. The ride is quiet and tired.
KAREN. The traffic gets worse as you get closer to the city.
PHIL. Then you skip more of the details as you tell more and more people, as I have.
AYUN. And then it's back to classes and rehearsal.
KAREN. And then it's your turn to the dishes.
AYUN. Then I didn't make this phone call.
KAREN. And I'm staying at my girlfriend's tonight.
AYUN. Then where did you put that album I lent you?
KAREN. And stay out of my room.
AYUN. Well you're never here anyway.
KAREN. I pay rent, too.
(This builds until they are both yelling at each other. Phil crawls back into the airplane and goes through the motions of skydiving.)
PHIL. Dot. Go. 1000 2000 3000 4000 5000 Look. Reach! PULL!
(As his chute opens Ayun & Karen's voices cease, their actions continue, and all we hear is the wind.)

CURTAIN

LYING IN THE DARK
©1992 by Dave Awl and Phil Ridarelli

(Dark stage.)

GREG K. Are you comfortable?
AYUN. Yeah. Sure.
(Beat.)
GREG K. Are you warm enough?
AYUN. I'm fine, thanks.
(Beat.)
GREG K. Look, I want to apologize for...
AYUN. No, that's o.k., you're here with me now. That's the important thing.
(Beat.)
TIM. Is everything all right here?
(Beat.)
AYUN. Actually, I was looking for something in a beige.
GREG A. *(Over microphone)* Illinois. YKU. one three six. Beige Mazda. Your lights are on. 10 9 8 7 6 5 4 3 2 10 9 8 7 6 ... *(Countdown continues throughout.)*
GREG K. Do you want me to get that?
AYUN. If they really want to talk to you they'll call back.
("Moonlight Serenade" begins playing.)
GREG K. Oh my God, honey, I left Mr. Harris in the waiting room. He's been there over an hour, honey.
AYUN. Don't worry, if he gets hungry he can kill a mouse or something, honey.
DAVE. *(Over the megaphone)* Honey. Honey. Honey. When the dog bites. When the bee stings. When I'm feeling...sad.
(Spencer and Lisa begin singing "Ring Around The Rosey." Phil begins barking. We hear a steady buzzing.)
HEATHER. I love the way the ocean looks at midnight. So peaceful. *(She strikes a match and immediately blows it out. She does this three times.)*
DAVE. *(Over the megaphone)* Honey, I'm worried about the new ranch-hand, Luke. He's been behaving rather oddly, don't you think.
KAREN. I'm getting tired. Can't we find a place to stop for the night?
HEATHER. You two make a beautiful couple.
GREG A. *(Over the microphone.)* 5 4 3 2 1. *("Ring Around the Rosey" ends with the end of the countdown. The last words being, "Ashes, ashes, we all fall..." Silence)*
GREG K. We're alone now.
AYUN. Just the two of us.

CURTAIN

MANIFEST DENSITY
©1991 by Greg Allen

Greg Allen stands on stage with a fist full of one dollar bills repeating "WHO WANTS A DOLLAR? WHO WANTS A DOLLAR? WHO WANTS A DOLLAR?" When he gets an audience member to volunteer he says, "COME UP HERE ON STAGE! COME RIGHT UP HERE ON STAGE! COME ON UP HERE!" When the audience volunteer comes up on stage he again asks them, "YOU WANT A DOLLAR? YOU WANT A DOLLAR? YOU WANT A DOLLAR?" If the audience member says "yes," Greg says "There's your dollar" and gives the person a dollar and they leave the stage. Greg again wanders around in front of the audience barking "WHO WANTS A DOLLAR? WHO WANTS A DOLLAR? WHO WANTS A DOLLAR?" He picks one of the audience volunteers (usually numerous at this point) and says, "COME UP HERE ON STAGE! COME RIGHT UP HERE ON STAGE!" When they come up on stage he again assaults them with "YOU WANT A DOLLAR? YOU WANT A DOLLAR? YOU WANT A DOLLAR?" If they say "yes", he says "Bark like a dog! Come on, bark like a dog! Bark like a dog!" If the person barks like a dog he gives them their dollar and congratulates them as they go back to their seat. Greg again returns to his chants of "WHO WANTS A DOLLAR!", gets another audience volunteer on stage and, after confirming that they want a dollar, says, "Show everyone your bellybutton! Show everyone in the audience your bellybutton! Come on, show us your bellybutton!" If the audience volunteer does so, they are given their dollar and congratulated. The process is repeated again until an audience member is on stage and it is confirmed that they want a dollar. Greg then says "Give me a kiss! Come on, give me a great big kiss right here on the mouth! Give me a kiss!" If the audience member does so (on the lips, none of this cheek business) they are given their dollar and congratulated and return to their seat. The process is repeated again with a little more avid "WHO WANTS A DOLLAR? WHO WANTS A DOLLAR? WHO WANTS A DOLLAR?" Another audience member takes the stage and confirms that they indeed do want a dollar. Greg then says, "Rip off your clothes! Just rip off all your clothes! Just rip 'em all off!" If the audience volunteer begins to disrobe they are encouraged with shouts of "RIP 'EM ALL OFF! ALL YOUR CLOTHES! RIGHT OFF! TAKE 'EM ALL OFF!" If, as some people are apt to do, they only go down to their underwear and stop there, Greg can offer them two and even three dollars, especially if the audience is encouraging this like rabid dogs around a toddler. If the audience member becomes completely nude they are dutifully given the money they were promised. At this point, or indeed at any point where Greg is given a clear refusal to go along with his demands, he turns to the audience and says, "America: Land of the Free, Home of the Brave."

CURTAIN

THE MEN'S MOVEMENT
©1992 by Greg Kotis

(Phil and Greg Kotis sit facing each other onstage. Their exchange of dialogue remains stiff and serious throughout the play. Their movements are kept to an absolute minimum.)

PHIL. I really like what you've done with your hair.
GREG. Thanks. *(Pause)* The guy who cut it did a really nice job. *(Pause)* I think.
PHIL. Yeah. *(Pause)* It's nice.
GREG. I don't have to do much with it. *(Pause)* I just shampoo, condition, and go. *(Pause)* You know what I mean?
PHIL. Sure. *(Pause)* Who has time now-a-days to fool around with mousse or gel or any of that.
GREG. Forget about it. *(Pause)* That's a nice look you've got going.
PHIL. Thanks. *(Pause)* It's functional too. *(Pause)* Easy to move around in.
GREG. That's great.
PHIL. Yeah. I, uh... *(Phil stops himself from speaking. Greg shuffles in his chair uncomfortably.)*
PHIL. I am the wind and the rain and my spirit pushes past the cold and the pale and this hunting ground is yet our hunting ground and my blade, my blade, my blade, my blade.
(Both remain silent for a few moments.)
PHIL. Know what I mean?
GREG. Yeah. *(Pause)* Absolutely.

CURTAIN

THE MINUTE ACTIVIST
©1992 by Ayun Halliday

(Ayun stands before the audience.)

AYUN. In today's confusing times, it is imperative that citizens make their views known by writing their elected officials. Such grassroots lobbying can actually influence politicians by letting them know where their constituents stand on various issues. Unfortunately, many people today find that their hectic schedules rarely allow them the extra time needed to dash off an original letter to their Congressman or Senator. Here's a timesaving hint to help those busy folks get their opinions across, too. One: pick a card, any card, that you have received in the mail recently. Try to pick one with a pretty cover. *(Phil enters, reading from a Hallmark style card shaped like a kitty cat.)*

PHIL. Dear Phil, thank you so much for the pretty pink sweater you sent me on my birthday. You always were extra-thoughtful. You make me feel like a princess! The weather is fine here. Grandpa sends his love. Hugs and kisses, Grandma.

AYUN. Now. With a bottle of Liquid Paper, carefully white out your name and the name of the sender. Scan the letter until you find a good place to insert your concern. White that space out, too. Now, simply go down the letter, filling in the appropriate names and the appropriate issue. Find an envelope of the proper size and mail your card off in a matter of minutes! *(Greg Kotis enters, reading from a kitty cat card identical to Phil's.)*

GREG. Dear Senator, Thank you so much for voting in favor of reforms which will reduce unnecessary experimentation on animals. You always were extra-thoughtful. You make me feel like a princess. The weather is fine here. Grandpa sends his love. Hugs and kisses, Phil Ridarelli.

AYUN. Everyone enjoys receiving festive greeting cards in the mail! Plus, you'll feel better knowing you took the extra time to make sure your voice is heard. *(Lisa enters, reading from a postcard.)*

LISA. Dear Senator, Florida is a blast, man! We get shit-faced every night and fry on the beach all day. Wish you were supporting legislation to overturn the Gag Rule! Love ya', Lisa Buscani. *(Dave enters, reading from a phone bill.)*

DAVE. Dear President Bush, this is the 4th notice you have received. Please reduce tax hikes and military spending immediately or call our office during business hours to discuss alternative arrangements. Dave Awl and the cast and crew of the Neo-Futurists. Say, I never knew recycling could be so much fun!

AYUN. That's right, Dave! Keep those cards and letters coming. And going!

CURTAIN

A MINUTE OF HOPE
©1989, 1992 by Greg Allen

(Heather and Greg Allen sit on stage. Greg is in a swivel chair with his back to the audience. Heather sits beside a small table with a phone into which she is speaking.)

HEATHER. Thank you. Goodbye. *(Hangs up.)* Hi, I'm Heather, a simulated receptionist down here at Backpat Industries. Stay tuned for an important offer that could make your life a whole lot easier.

GREG. *(Turning towards the audience, with compassion)* Hunger. Poverty. Homelessness. AIDS. These are just a few of the ever-growing, ever-troublesome concerns that threaten to upset our daily lives. But what can you, just one individual, do to help yourself overcome the plague which is sweeping across America known as "Nagging Liberal Guilt". This once every commercial break offer, finally gives you the opportunity to put those hard earned dollars to good use, alleviating your conscience forever for when you walk by the outstretched hands of foul-smelling degenerate lunatics. Here's well-paid actress Brooke Shields to tell you more.

(Ayun walks on with Spencer who has a cup full of water and a spoon with which she creates constant tears by hurling water into Ayun's eyes.)

AYUN. *(Frantic)* I was so confused and upset I didn't know what to do. I heard about all these people in Australia starving to death with no food and no water and saw pictures of little tiny girls and babies with open mouths crying out for anything they could possibly even get the slightest malnourishment from...

GREG. That's Somalia, Brooke.

AYUN. Oh what's the difference? They were starving and I was so upset I couldn't model and I was losing hundreds of thousands of dollars and I was so upset I didn't know what to do I didn't know what to do I didn't know what... *(Spencer slaps her.)*

AYUN. *(Calmed)* Thanks, Mom. And then I found Guilt Away. And made this commercial.

KOTIS. *(Emerging from the wings)* Thanks, Brooke. Yes, here at Guilt Away we take care of every liberal social concern you could possibly think of. In addition to world hunger, poverty, homelessness, and the other biggies, we cover gun control, No Nukes, and AIDS. We've got whales, animal rights, and rain forests for the environmentalists, abortion and ERA for the ladies, divestment for you blacks, and gay rights for the homosexuals. Hell, we even give a few bucks to Jerry's kids. And what would you expect to pay for this amazing offer? A hundred dollars? One hundred and fifty dollars? Two hundred dollars? No, a hundred and fifty dollars is all it takes to get these monkeys permanently off your back.

PHIL. *(Emerging from upstage and charging down towards the audience)* But wait, there's more! You've heard about all the hubbub in Europe, those crazy commies duking for democracy? Well if you act now you'll get one genuine imitation blood splattered t-shirt right off the back of some poor fool who actually stood up and fought for his human rights. Yes, what a conversation piece. You're thinking "For just a hundred and fifty bucks I get all this?" YES! And that's not all. If you call now before I stop speaking you will receive one pathetic photograph of an actual under-privileged third-world child knocking at death's door. It's ripe for framing and laminated with tear-resistant gloss. "How can they do it?" you say? Fuck if I know, I'm just a salesman.

GREG. *(Sensitively)* Think ... of the children, the whales, that bag lady you accidentally tripped on the way to work today. Feel bad? Help yourself. Open your heart. Open your wallet.

HEATHER. Hi, I'm Heather, a simulated receptionist down here at Backpat Industries. If you'd like to take advantage of the important offer Ms. Shields tried to speak of, simply call 275-5255 and some underpaid illegal alien will be there to answer your call. Call now and receive this special membership button: "I Gave, So Fuck Off". I'm waiting for my residuals. Please call now.

CURTAIN

MISGIVEN
©1992 by Heather Riordan

(The play takes place in the dark. There is a bright light shining in from the double doors.)

PHIL. The child was outside my window
SCOTT. the child was drooling
HEATHER. the child was outside my bedroom window
AYUN. the child had one of those murderous zombie expressions
GREG K. standing on the window ledge
PHIL. his eyes never
SCOTT. they never
HEATHER. his eyes never blinked
AYUN. he was holding a rock
GREG. holding a huge rock over his head
HEATHER. I could tell from where I was, on the bed, that he meant me harm
SCOTT. he would touch the rock to the window, and then lean back as if to
AYUN. shatter the window
GREG K. to come in
PHIL. shatter the window
HEATHER. to come in
SCOTT. to come inside.
AYUN. I almost
GREG K. I
PHIL. I almost let him in
HEATHER. the child said:
SCOTT. let me inside. I need to get back inside. It's my place, really. It's my right. I should be free to come in. You had no right. You had no right at all.
AYUN. I asked him to put down the rock
GREG K. he said he couldn't—the rock signified too much, too much of something I didn't understand
PHIL. I almost let him in *(Heather crosses towards door standing in the light.)*
HEATHER. I went towards the window, pretending to be about to let him in—and pushed the fan through the window, pushing him off the ledge, pushing him down, pushing it all down with the shattered glass to the garden three flights below *(Heather slams doors shut.)*
HEATHER. the room's been so cold since then.

CURTAIN

MISS MARY MACK
©1990 by Lisa Buscani

(Lisa and Karen sit center stage, and clap hands together. The "Miss Mary Mack" routine is appropriate.)

LISA. Nadine held my hand when we were kids.
When she stopped I thought she didn't love me anymore.
KAREN. Can I braid your hair?
LISA. We used to call my grandma "the hoover,"
because her kisses were like a vacuum.
KAREN. I love you, a bushel and a peck, a bushel and a peck,
And a hug around the neck . . .
LISA. When I lost my virginity in a less than romantic manner, Fiona put the tea pot on.
KAREN. He's an asshole. Need a hug?
LISA. Val took me to the campus clinic. They had a VHF Viewmaster that showed the pap smear process up close and personal.
KAREN. Maybe we should tone it down a bit . . .
LISA. When her husband died, Mrs. Goldberg broke down over the thought of going on their upcoming trip to Europe solo.
KAREN. I held her. She felt small.
LISA. I lay in my mother's bed, it was her bed then, and I told her I was ugly and nobody liked me. *(Karen grabs Lisa's hands.)*
KAREN. My darling, you will always be beautiful to me.

CURTAIN

MORE NEWS FROM THE ART WORLD
©1991 by Tim Reinhard

(Tim and Spencer sit facing out toward the audience.)

TIM. Good evening and welcome to More News from the Art World. For Friday, October 25, 1991, I'm Tim Reinhard.

SPENCER. And I'm Spencer Kayden. Our top story tonight comes from Killeen, Texas, where a one time performance is causing a lot of unrest in the community and a lot of questions about the artist. The artist is 35 year old George Hennard, and his latest piece called "Worst Mass Shooting in U.S. History" is a mix of guerilla theatre, live ammunition and innocent bystanders. Hennard and his performance received national attention as he smashed his pick-up truck into a restaurant at lunchtime, stepped out of the cab, and opened fire with a semi-automatic pistol killing 22 people before killing himself.

(Tim and Spencer turn toward each other to discuss the story.)

TIM. Well, I really liked it. The piece is so rich, it's really dense, it's got a lot in it and it says a lot of great things. Hennard has a line right before he opens fire, he says "This is what Bell County has done to me." That would almost be too much if it weren't followed by such a heinous act, but he pulls it off really well. And I think in that one line is encapsulated the point of the piece. It clearly speaks to his immense frustration and his feelings of absolute helplessness and victimization by the rest of society.

SPENCER. It's very reminiscent of the work of Lauri Dann or the Austin sniper in the late '60s.

TIM. Very similar. Different weapons, different location, but the point of the piece is in the same vein and is just as timely today as those other works you mentioned.

SPENCER. I liked it too. I didn't think I was going to. It started off as just another one of those "guy can't get his life together, feels victimized by society, goes out and shoots a bunch of people". But, he chose Luby's, the most crowded restaurant in town and it was Bosses' Day. I don't know what that means, but I like it. It adds a layer of...

TIM. I know what you mean. The whole piece is full of those little moments, little fragmented instances which keep a pressure cooker feeling, and really say "hey this is really a madman here." So it's gruesome, horrific, terrifying, but very clear and says some great things, and certainly lives up to the title. I give it high marks. *(Tim and Spencer face the audience.)* Well, that's all the time we've got. We'll be back next week with More News From the Art World, and until then, get out your art supplies and make the world the way you want it. I'm Tim Reinhard.

SPENCER. And I'm Spencer Kayden.

TIM & SPENCER. Goodnight.

CURTAIN

MOVING TARGETS
©1990 by Heather Riordan

(Heather is facing audience, with a bright red lipstick in hand. She draws a large circle on Ayun's back who is seated facing upstage, with her bare back to audience. Between each of her lines, Heather draws a smaller circle on Ayun's back, making a bullseye.)

HEATHER. A lot of women who've been raped are coming forward with their stories in the hope that people will realize how widespread sexual assault is. I thought this was a good idea. I thought this would help me.

TED. You really can't prove it was rape—she let him in.

HEATHER. I found instead, that people have a need to find fault with the victim, so they can go on believing it can't happen to them.

SPENCER. Look at the way she was dressed—she shouldn't go around flaunting her body like that.

HEATHER. Usually, one of the first questions was what was I wearing. One person asked me if I was dressed in such a manner that would invite such an attack. Like what, wearing a t-shirt that says please rape me?

LISA. I'm not saying it was her fault, but what was she doing in Central Park that late?

HEATHER. She was jogging!

KAREN. It's a biological urge.

HEATHER. A friend of mine's grandmother was attacked in her own back yard. She's afraid to go outside because the guy said he'd be back to kill her.

BETSY. You take your chances living in the city.

HEATHER. I thought it would be very healing to share my experience. It was like being raped all over again.

CURTAIN

NO TECH! NO TECH!
©1992 by Greg Kotis

(Greg Kotis is left alone kneeling on stage after a moment of convincing pre-play set up chaos which includes blacking out the theater. A few beats after "go" is called, Greg K. says to Razor, the light booth operator,...)

GREG K. We need some stage lights here, Razor.
RAZOR. I know, I'm getting it. *(Several seconds pass.)*
GREG K. Time is of the essence, Razor, let's go!
RAZOR. I said I'm getting it. Relax. *(Several seconds pass.)*
GREG K. All right, what the fuck is going on up there?!
LISA. Calm down, Greg, she's working on it.
GREG K. You calm down, Lisa, my play is being fucked up because we can't seem to light the fucking stage.
GREG A. Maybe we should move on and come back to this play when we've figured out what's wrong with the lights.
GREG K. No! No way, Greg. Not this time. *(Turns on a flashlight and directs it toward the booth.)* Razor, how are you doing up there?
RAZOR. I'm working on it!
GREG K. Jesus fucking christ!
PHIL. Here, let me see if I can help. *(Phil turns on flashlight and proceeds toward the booth.)*
GREG K. Stay where you are! *(Phil stops and directs his flashlight towards Greg K. who is revealed holding a gun.)*
AYUN. Oh my God, he has a gun!
GREG K. That's right! And unless I get some tech RIGHT NOW there's gonna be trouble!
DAVE. Jesus, Greg, she's working on it. *(Greg directs his flashlight towards Dave.)*
HEATHER. Yeah, Greg, she's doing the best she can. *(Greg directs his flashlight towards Heather.)*
GREG A. So why don't you put the gun down. *(Greg directs his flashlight towards Greg A. who is revealed holding a gun.)*
AYUN. Oh my God, he has a gun too!
LISA. That's right, Greg, just put the gun down and we'll...have a little talk. *(Greg directs his flashlight towards Lisa who is revealed holding a gun.)*
AYUN. Oh my God, SHE has a gun!
LISA. Can it, Ayun, so do you.
AYUN. Oh yeah...right... *(Ayun turns on her flashlight and directs it toward Greg K.)*
PHIL. That's right, Greg we all have guns now. *(Heather turns on her flashlight and directs it toward Greg K.)*
HEATHER. So why don't you put the gun down, Greg? *(Dave turns on his flashlight and directs it toward Greg K.)*
DAVE. Try and cooperate, Greg. You're only making it harder on yourself. *(All descend toward the stage, lights directed toward Greg K.)*
GREG K. *(Greg K. collapses.)* But...but...my play...time is of the essence...oh, Jesus Jesus Jesus.
RAZOR. All right, I got them!!
GREG A. Everyone clear the stage. *(Everyone does.)* Ready? "No Tech! No Tech!" Go! *(Lights up on Greg K. who is left alone kneeling center stage.)*
GREG K. Jesus Jesus Jesus.

CURTAIN.

P.P.S.I.L.O.V.E.Y.O.U.
©1991 by Heather Riordan and John Funk

(Four chairs are placed center stage facing in a straight line the audience. A water bottle is placed on each chair. In unison, Heather, Greg K., Ayun, and Phil enter, stand beside a chair, pick up a bottle, open the bottle, drink, put the bottle down, lie in front of their chair, stand up, and exit. This action takes place while the following text is read over the microphone.)

SCOTT. Hottest bitch, receive this long distance kiss, swoon from its hot whiskey breath. The heat has finally broken, the rancid weight of the past weeks lifted away—the magician's scarf as he reveals the dove. Naturally, I thought of you. I hear that you're very busy and very broke. May I pass on some advice from Truman Capote? Get yourself a personal maid. Go into hock and hire yourself some exotic thing to run your bath and turn down your bed. You'll feel loved and pampered, your fortunes will rise, your outlook will change completely. I'm thinking of us on the beach that day, at Oak Street. Remember, the Evian, and that really attractive teenager, with the leg brace? There is no beach here, no Evian. There are teenagers, but their prices never drop till after four, till they're looking for a warm bed. Ask around. Yours like a woodland friend in a snare.

CURTAIN

A PRAYER
©1991 by Lisa Buscani

(Entire cast on stage in various lying/standing positions with candles.)

HEATHER.
You
rage-cropped father,
DAVE.
You
earth-stained mother,
GREG A.
You
Flaming spirit,
GREG K.
You
laughing jackal,
LISA.
You
rising bird,
PHIL.
You
knowing shadow,
AYUN.
You
inner being *(Pause.)*
GREG A.
I won't kneel
that will bring me closer
to what defeats me now
GREG K.
I won't bow
because I can't cower
in the face of a question
AYUN.
But I can ask
and hear my plea flood the air
and take comfort in the fact
that I still have the strength
to want *(Pause.)*
PHIL.
I am so tired.
Cliches about weight aside,
The world has nested on my shoulders,
settling down for a long winter's nap.
HEATHER.
My life follows the coldest road,
Dark and indifferent,
and quite happy to roll on without me.
DAVE.
And sometimes I feel like I'm the only rider

that rests in me so heavily
that all I can do is sit down
and hope for a still moment.
GREG A.
When I look to the light of the future
I see no bright goal
only that same road
that forgets the sound of my steps.
LISA.
You who know the true meaning of beyond,
You who hold the lives of so many people
in your strange justice,
You who promise this life will be justified,
Send some of that folky old narcotic my way,
can't ya?
And let me step back awhile.
GREG A.
I ask for peace,
PHIL.
I ask for patience,
HEATHER.
I ask for health,
GREG K.
I ask for truth,
AYUN.
I ask for beauty,
LISA.
I ask for company,
DAVE.
I ask for love. *(Pause.)*
AYUN.
Amen
GREG K.
Omen
LISA.
Whatever.

CURTAIN

PRETZEL, PRETZEL
©1991 by Greg Kotis

(Tim and Greg stand several yards apart center stage. Tim is eating a pretzel. Greg is not.)

GREG. Looks like you've got yourself a nice little snack.
TIM. Yes. I have a snack.
GREG. Nice.
TIM. Sure.
GREG. Salty. Crunchy. Tasty. Nice.
TIM. Maybe you should get yourself one. Maybe you should get yourself a pretzel. To eat.
GREG. I would like to have one. To eat. I feel...seeing you eat the pretzel...I feel...unoccupied. Inert. Like the pretzel itself. Not having a pretzel to eat I feel like I am a pretzel.
TIM. Yes. It's so tasty. The pretzel. So good to eat now.
GREG. Nice.
TIM. Sure.
GREG. Give that pretzel to me now. Give it to me to eat. *(Pause.)* Kidding.
TIM. You really had me going there for a moment.
GREG. Yes.
TIM. The way you had me going for a moment, that's your pretzel I think. When you get me going you're having a nice little snack.
GREG. Give that pretzel to me now. Give it to me to eat. *(Pause.)*
TIM. You really had me going there for a moment.
GREG. Yes.
TIM. Nice.
GREG. Sure.

CURTAIN

PUBLIC ADDRESS
©1989 by Karen Christopher

KAREN. I once gave a bum my phone number.

ROBIN. Four score and seven years ago our fathers brought forth on this continent a new nation...

KAREN. I didn't mean to I mean it wasn't my intention but then he asked me for it and he was reciting the Gettysburg Address and I thought: He could be my father. So I gave him my phone number so he could call me when he needed a ride or something.

ROBIN. ...conceived in liberty and dedicated to the proposition that all men are created equal.

KAREN. Harry, that was his name Harry, he said people were always taking advantage of him. He was holding a little bottle of whiskey in a bag and he smelled like rotting polyester. He was 76 years old, that's what he told me. When I got home and told my boyfriend I'd given a bum my phone number I realized I'd made a mistake.

ROBIN. The world will little note nor long remember what we say here but it can never forget what they did here.

KAREN. The next day Harry called me from the Red Onion. I told him I was sorry but he should lose my number and not ever call again. I felt bad.

ROBIN. ...that we here highly resolve the these men shall not have died in vain...

KAREN. He called once more about a month later, he left a message on the machine he said: Hi Karen, I'm in the JC Penny's. Call me here or just come down, sporting goods department.

ROBIN. ...That this nation, under God, shall have a new birth of freedom, and that government of the people, by the people, for the people shall not perish from the Earth.

CURTAIN

THE RAGGEDY ANN AND GREG SHOW
©1992 by Greg Kotis and Dave Awl

(Greg Kotis sits onstage with a "Raggedy Ann" doll seated on his lap. Throughout the play, Greg supplies the voice and movements of Raggedy Ann.)

GREG. Well, Raggedy Ann, tonight I thought we might talk to the folks in the audience about something which seems to be on everyone's mind. And that something is "family values". *(To the audience)* Can we all say that together? FAMILY VALUES. Good.

RAGGEDY ANN. Well, you know Greg, I come from a time when boys and girls would reach out to the values I symbolized: play nice, be friendly, and maintain the family unit. Can we all say that together? MAINTAIN THE FAMILY UNIT. Good. But sometimes I think that my voice is too little, too gentle, and too kind to be heard next to the big and loud voices of those who don't have family values. And that makes me sad.

GREG. That makes me sad, too, Raggedy Ann. Well, why don't we bring out someone who has some of his own ideas about family values.

RAGGEDY ANN. I hope they're not different from mine!

GREG. Ha ha ha ha...

ANN. Ha ha ha ha...

GREG. Ha ha ha ha...

ANN. Ha ha ha ha...

GREG. Dave, come on over and join us, won't you? *(Dave enters and sits with Greg and Ann.)*

DAVE. Hi, Greg.

GREG. Hi, Dave.

DAVE. Hi, Raggedy Ann.

ANN. Hi, Dave.

GREG. Tonight we're talking about "family values". Could you share with us some of your own thoughts about "family values"?

DAVE. Sure, Greg. I think Love is at the center of what families are all about. I mean, I think a family is basically a group of people who support and take care of each other regardless of what differences they may have.

RAGGEDY ANN. "Differences?"

GREG. Well, I think Dave's talking about being gay.

DAVE. Right. And having the support of a family has helped me survive as a gay person and cope with the stress of being different in a sometimes hostile world.

RAGGEDY ANN. Now, wait a minute, Dave. America was created by millions of families struggling to create a better life for their children. And by family I mean a mommy and a daddy who are married to each other and have boys and girls who will some day grow up to be mommies and daddies and have boys and girls of their own.

DAVE. Well, Raggedy Ann, that's one kind of family and it can be a good kind of family but it's not the only kind of family there is. Life isn't always perfect, Raggedy Ann, and in reality families come in all different shapes and sizes. And as long as those families take care of each other and support each other then I think they're good families.

RAGGEDY ANN. I don't think promoting homosexuality is a good way to maintain the family unit.

DAVE. Well, how does it strengthen the family unit to throw people out of families just because they don't fit some model of the ideal family? When I came out to my family they accepted me and that's made our family stronger than it was before.

RAGGEDY ANN. Well, you think it's stronger because your homosexual mind has twisted your parents' frowns of unhappiness into evil smiles of acceptance. That's just part of your diseased militant agenda that gnaws like a cancer at the heart of the American family. Can we all say that together? YOUR DISEASED MILITANT AGENDA THAT GNAWS LIKE A CANCER AT THE HEART OF THE AMERICAN FAMILY.

DAVE. Well, Raggedy Ann, what I think is gnawing at the heart of the American family is fear and prejudice.

RAGGEDY ANN. What are you talking about, Dave?

DAVE. Oh come on Rags, it's pretty obvious you wouldn't be here tonight if you weren't afraid that your phony cardboard apple pie image of America is being exposed for the sham it is. You're afraid, so you want everyone else to be afraid, too. Can we all say that together, please?

RAGGEDY ANN. No! No, we can't all say that together. You're right Dave, I am afraid because anything that doesn't stand for the family stands against it.

DAVE. Raggedy Ann, I'm proud of who I am and I see no reason to hide it!

RAGGEDY ANN. Faggot! *(Raggedy Ann struggles while Greg K. attempts to silence her.)*

GREG. Well, that's all the time we have folks. And remember, there's a little bit of Raggedy Ann in all of us.

CURTAIN

RAPE
©1990 by Ayun Halliday

(Ayun, Lisa, Ted & Phil sit onstage.)

LISA. I was walking back from the grocery yesterday and about a block from my home, this guy leaned out of his car and started whistling and saying all this stuff to me and he wouldn't stop. I felt like I was being raped.

PHIL. I got to the office yesterday and my desk, I could tell just by looking at it, somebody had been rummaging around in my desk, my papers and everything! I felt just like I'd been raped.

TED. I had a friend over to my place the other day and I got a long distance telephone call. So I went into the other room and when I came back, my friend was reading my mail, my personal mail! I felt like I'd been raped.

LISA. You really do.

PHIL. You do.

TED. It's exactly like being raped.

AYUN. The victim, 27 years old, was found locked in the trunk of her car, with a pair of pantyhose knotted tightly around her neck and a pair of nylon bikini panties stuffed down her throat. Her hands were bound behind her back with a length of telephone cord. The victim was nude. Her head, face, and upper torso were badly bruised, and there were cigarette burns on her breasts and inner thighs. Scratch marks on the victim's body and in the area surrounding the car indicate a struggle. The county coroner is completing tests to determine if the victim was raped, as the night before the abduction was her first year anniversary and she and her husband had engaged in sexual intercourse.

LISA. I felt extremely violated.

PHIL. I felt like I'd been violated in the worst possible way.

TED. I felt like I'd been raped.

CURTAIN

REALLY, REALLY LITTLE
©1992 by Greg Kotis

(Greg Kotis, Heather, and Phil stand on stage. They punctuate their lines with large choreographed gestures.)

ALL. We mortals!
We little people!
Give thanks!
To the Pantheon of the Gods!
KOTIS. Composed of some of the most...
HEATHER. Intriguing!
ALL. And!
PHIL. Compelling!
KOTIS. Personalities of our day and age. We...
ALL. Little people!
KOTIS. Would just like to...
ALL. Express!
KOTIS. Once again, our undying devotion to the...
ALL. Residents of the Pantheon of the Gods!
KOTIS. Including...
HEATHER. Madonna!
PHIL. The Goddess of Love!
KOTIS. General Norman Schwarzkopf!
HEATHER. The God of War!
PHIL. Michael Jordan!
KOTIS. The God of Basketball! And many...
HEATHER. Many!
PHIL. Many!
KOTIS. Many!
HEATHER. Many!
PHIL. Many!
KOTIS. Many more! Just listen to what some of these...
ALL. Little people!!
KOTIS. Have to say about the divine personalties we get to share this planet with: *(Kotis, Heather, and Phil slap the floor rhythmically to provide an exciting backdrop to the following testimony. Dave enters and stands center stage.)*
DAVE. *(Cheerfully)* Robert DeNiro? What an actor! My God, if I had just a little tiny smidgen of a fraction of what he has in terms of presence and mystery and potency I'd consider my life worth living! It's all so hopeless, isn't it? And Bobby reminds me of that every time he walks in front of a camera. And when I walk out of that theater I feel really, really small, like about this big. Thanks Bobby! *(Dave exits. Ayun takes his place center stage.)*
AYUN. *(With great excitement.)* Yoko Ono? My God, not only does she live in the Dakota but she's one of the foremost artists of our time, continually redefining how we think about art, music, and John Lennon! Of course I have my bagel. Would anyone like to see it? *(Ayun frowns and exits. Greg A. takes her place.)*
GREG A. I can do this thing with my back where...never mind. *(Greg A. exits. Kotis, Heather, and Phil stop slapping the floor.)*
ALL. Yes!
KOTIS. Even during times as difficult as these it's...
ALL. Good!

KOTIS. To know that in cities like...
HEATHER. Hollywood, California!
KOTIS. And...
PHIL. New York City, New York!
KOTIS. There are people bigger than life that we get to see every day on...
ALL. Television!
KOTIS. And read about in magazines like...
ALL. Rolling Stone!
KOTIS. And...
ALL. Newsweek!
KOTIS. That make us all feel...
ALL. Really, really little!!
KOTIS. We thank you.

CURTAIN

RED LIGHT, GREEN LIGHT
©1992 by Lisa Buscani

(Ensemble stands on stage playing a game of "Red Light, Green Light." Lisa stands downstage center.)

LISA. You live in an OK part of town and go to an OK school because your dad has an OK job that doesn't pay him a whole lot of money. Your grades are OK. They'd be better if your lessons were more interesting, but your teachers don't seem to care as much because their salary is less than OK. You apply for college but your SATs and ACTs are just OK because you didn't have the money or the time to take those standardized testing classes because you have to work. You don't mind, that's OK. Your parents can't afford the one really good school you get into, so you settle for a smaller local school that is OK. Your grades are OK. They'd be better, but you have to work because your parents can't afford to give you much money. You don't mind, that's OK. When you get out, you apply for jobs, but all the really good jobs that you're interested in go to the kids from the really good schools with the really good grades. You get a job that's OK. You find somebody and get married. You live in an OK part of town and send your kids to an OK school because you have an OK job that doesn't pay you a whole lot of money . . . *(Lisa is forced to go back to the starting line.)* It's OK. Really.

CURTAIN

REMBRANDT
©1992 by Ayun Halliday

(Ayun and Greg Allen sit, examining a Barbie and G.I. Joe, respectively. Phil stands between them, behind a mysterious shoebox.)

AYUN. Fashion toys like Barbie only teach children an impossibly high standard of beauty and fool them into thinking that the more clothes you have, the more popular you'll be...

GREG. Whereas war toys like G.I. Joe and Rambo only encourage children to act aggressively and settle their differences through violence.

PHIL. Looking for an educational doll that's as glamorous as Barbie and as rugged as G.I. Joe without all the disagreeable psychic baggage they inevitably carry?

AYUN & GREG. Yes!!!

(Phil produces a Barbie tarted up in 17th century garb from the depths of the shoebox.)

PHIL. Kids just love playing with Rembrandt Harmenzoon Van Rijn from Toy-co.

AYUN. Rembrandt Harmenzoon Van Rijn? Say, wasn't he the famous 17th century Dutch painter who produced over 300 etchings between 1626 and 1665?

PHIL. That's right. Your kids'll love collecting Rembrandt's etching trading cards. We've got all the biggies: "Descent from the Cross," "The Stoning of St. Stephen," "The Baptism of the Eunuch," and of course, "The Circumcision in the Stable." Each etching card has a Rembrandt fun fact on the back. Swap 'em with your buddies!

GREG. *(Examining trading card)* It says here that in 1650, Rembrandt had his mistress Geertje Direx put away in a penal institution, apparently in order to evade most of his obligations to her...

AYUN. *(Examining doll)* Hey! What's this cord for?

PHIL. Pull it and see. *(Ayun pulls cord on Rembrandt doll's back.)*

DAVE. *(On microphone)* Under my hand the quality of etched lines and tints was turned into a revelatory vehicle!

GREG. Let me try!

DAVE. *(On microphone)* What shall I wear to the dance in the Leidsplein tonight? Perhaps my heavy fur cap and my embroidered cloak.

PHIL. Besides all of his great clothes, you'll want to make sure you collect all of Rembrandt's accessories.

AYUN. Wow! Etching tools!

GREG. A self-portrait!

PHIL. Don't forget the dream-house and Rembrandt's pony, Nugget.

SPENCER. *(Entering)* I love to comb his pretty hair.

PHIL. He's sexier than Barbie and his etchings are every bit as bloody as any havoc wreaked by Rambo. No well-cultured child should be without him.

SPENCER. Rembrandt Harmenzoon Van Rijn, I love you!!!

ALL. Awww.....

CURTAIN

REVOLUTION
©1990 by Greg Allen

(An off-stage narrator calls the numbers of the sections.)

NARRATOR. One:
HEATHER. Get out!
GREG. What are you talking about?
HEATHER. Get out!
GREG. But I love you.
HEATHER. Well I don't love you. It's over.
NARRATOR. Two:
GREG. Don't go.
HEATHER. This can't go on.
GREG. Yes it can.
HEATHER. No, I won't let it.
GREG. We can work things out.
HEATHER. Why don't you just leave?
GREG. I love you.
HEATHER. Get out!
GREG. What are you talking about?
HEATHER. Get out!
GREG. But I love you.
HEATHER. Well I don't love you. It's over.
NARRATOR. Three:
GREG. Wait, I don't know what's going on.
HEATHER. I'm leaving, that's what's going on.
GREG. But ... oh God, I'm losing my mind.
HEATHER. You're losing a lot more than that.
GREG. I don't want to.
HEATHER. That's what you say now, but what about in five minutes from now?
GREG. Don't go.
HEATHER. This can't go on.
GREG. Yes it can.
HEATHER. No, I won't let it.
GREG. We can work things out.
HEATHER. Why don't you just leave?
GREG. I love you.
NARRATOR. Four:
HEATHER. How could you ... you just don't care anymore. You haven't put a single ounce of effort into making this work. ... Well, all right, I'm leaving.
GREG. Wait, I don't know what's going on.
HEATHER. I'm leaving, that's what's going on.
GREG. But ... oh God, I'm losing my mind.
HEATHER. You're losing a lot more than that.
GREG. I don't want to.
HEATHER. That's what you say now, but what about in five minutes from now?
NARRATOR. Five:
GREG. Get out!
HEATHER. What are you talking about?

GREG. Get out!

HEATHER. But I love you.

GREG. Well I don't love you. It's over.

HEATHER. How could you ... you just don't care anymore. You haven't put a single ounce of effort into making this work. ... Well, all right, I'm leaving.

CURTAIN

*Note on staging:** Each segment of dialogue keeps the same blocking when repeated. Hence, during the announced numbers of the sections, the performers move to the starting position of the next section, dropping "character". *(In rehearsal I found it easiest to block the play chronologically and then reverse it.)* The performers' positions for the first and fifth sections are reversed, as is their dialogue.

RUDE POETRY
©1989 by Lisa Buscani and Bruce Neal

(Phil and Karen stand five feet apart, facing the audience. Lisa stands upstage and in between them with her back to the audience. Phil and Karen turn in to one another, push hands together and away from one another.)

PHIL & KAREN. *(In sing-songy, poetry voice.)* Get out of my way, you stupid mother-fucker. *(They begin to perform obnoxious, self-indulgent, modern dance-type movement while repeating this line. The line varies in pace, volume and pitch, and is repeated three times. When finished, man and woman dramatically throw themselves down, side-by-side, face to the floor.)*
LISA. *(Turning to face the audience.)*
I stepped into the elevator
And I stepped on her foot,
And she yelped like a dog,
And I said I was sorry, *(Phil and Karen look up to the audience.)*
But I wasn't.

CURTAIN

THE SANDS OF TIME
©1991 by Betsy Freytag

(Betsy is sitting center stage with a bucket of sand and is spooning out cupfuls of sand onto the floor after each statement. Different amounts for each statement.)

BETSY. I've been smoking for more than half my lifetime. I started drinking when I was eleven...and I haven't stopped. My friends say I drive like a maniac...maybe. I weighed in at 205 when I graduated from college. I, Betsy Freytag, hold harmless the aforementioned physician should pregnancy termination procedures result in complications, infertility or death... I love cheetos. There's a history of cancer in my family. It's been a long time since a man said "I love you"...it's taken it's toll. I do this thing a lot where I drink too fast and my soda or milk or whatever shoots through my nose...but I don't think that counts. I can live with that. *(Betsy stands holding the bucket. There is a hole in the bottom or the bucket and the remaining sand begins to flow out uncontrollably throughout the rest of the text.)*
A regular checkup, standard examination, massive lumps in both breasts, further analysis, an irregularity in the cervical cells, more tests, shot out of the stirrups, no answers, second opinions, more tests, insert the microscope, valium, waiting, improper structure, hormone pills, back on the table, waiting, back to the lab, no clear answers, back to the beginning, waiting, endless possibilities...27 years old...and I thought I had time to waste.

CURTAIN

SHE DON'T SELL NO SEASHELLS
©1992 by Karen Christopher

(Karen is lying on her back with her feet upstage. Legs are spread apart, knees up. She takes several short, sharp breaths. She takes a big one and begins the text - the text is to be delivered on one breath. She stops short twice only making it through to the end of the text on the third repetition. After second repetition Greg K. and Scott lift Karen by her knees so that she is hanging upside-down facing the audience. They are facing upstage.)

TEXT.
He doesn't think she'll be a good mother
He doesn't think she's old enough
He doesn't think she can manage a job and a child
He doesn't think she should get that tattoo she's been talking about
He doesn't want custody of their child
He doesn't want to be tied down like that

CURTAIN

SIT BACK AND RELAX
©1991 by Spencer Kayden and Greg Allen

(The theatre is completely dark. A pleasant voice is heard over a microphone.)

SPENCER. Ladies and gentlemen, while we want you to have a pleasant and enjoyable evening, the Neo-Futurists are also concerned about your safety. Smoking and drinking are not permitted in the theater and please refrain from talking during the performance as it could inhibit the total enjoyment of the theatrical experience of those around you. In the event of a natural disaster such as earthquake, tornado, or nuclear explosion, please remain in your seats at all times and we will inform you as to the extent of the damage at the end of the next play. The theatre is not scheduled to pass over any large bodies of water during the next hour, but if a nautical landing were attempted, the person next to you is your best bet as a flotation device. At this time we would like you to please reach over and hold the left hand of the audience member on your right. Go ahead. Don't be afraid. You have five seconds to comply.
(Actors in house yell "5-4-3-2-1!!!," while panning the audience with flashlights.)
Thank you. While holding this person's hand, ask yourself the following questions:
1) Did I come here with this person?
2) How well do I really know this person?
3) Would I trust this person with my life?
4) What does this person do with this hand that I would rather not know about?
Now please remove your hand and kindly refrain from touching anyone while you remain on the premises. At this time please remove all of your personal belongings from the area of the floor surrounding your seat and clench them tightly in your lap. We ask that you keep them in this position for the duration of the show. The Neo-Futurists will now inspect the aisles and any unclaimed property will be confiscated and destroyed.
(Using flashlights, the cast moves through the audience and brings any coats and bags they find onto the stage.)
I repeat any unclaimed property will be confiscated and destroyed. If you remember these simple guidelines for behavior while in the theatre — or for that matter, at home, at the office, or at social gatherings — your life will be made much more secure, safe, and sanitary. We thank you for your cooperation. Shut up and enjoy the show.

CURTAIN

SO, WHY THE ACCENT?
©1992 by Heather Riordan

(During the following play, the only lights are flashlights, which are manipulated in various ways by Ayun, Greg K., and Heather — e.g., circling around the actor, spinning on the floor, etc.)

AYUN. ze light
GREG K. ze light
HEATHER. step into ze light
AYUN. ze light
GREG K. ze light
HEATHER. do you see ze light
AYUN. ze light
GREG K. I have seen ze light
HEATHER. ze light
AYUN. ze light at ze end of ze tunnel
GREG K. ze light
HEATHER. turn off ze light
AYUN. ze light *(Ayun turns off her flashlight.)*
GREG K. turn off ze light *(Greg K. turns of his flashlight.)*
HEATHER. turn off ze light and come to bed.
(Heather turns off her flashlight.)

CURTAIN

SOMEONE TOLD ME WHEN YOU WAKE UP IN THE MORNING YOU SHOULD JUST BE HAPPY YOU'RE ALIVE

©1991 by Karen Christopher

(People alternate between looking at audience during song and bumping around like atoms during the talk.)

TED. What time is it?

GREG A. *(Answers.)*

KAREN. Help me.

CHORUS. Bum bum bum Son let me tell you 'bout a man named Jed...

TED. I can't go a day without biting my fingernails.

GREG A. Light bulbs were three for a dollar today at Walgreens.

KAREN. The baby was found in a plastic bag in the dumpster...etc.

CHORUS. ...poor mountaineer barely kept his family fed, then one day he was shootin' at some food...

TED. I was thinking, do I have to floss my teeth every night?

GREG A. When will I ever vacuum the house?

KAREN. He'd like to hit the man who begs for change by the cash station.

CHORUS. and up from the ground came a bubbling crude

TED. I just got an American Express card.

GREG A. My job is just running me ragged, I hate my boss.

KAREN. She doesn't understand this war thing but she definitely supported our troops.

CHORUS. Oil, that is, black gold, Texas tea...

TED. I'm always so tired I just don't know why I just can't get up about anything.

GREG A. I'm just waiting for something to happen.

CHORUS. Well the next thing you know old Jed's a millionaire kin folks said Jed move away from there, California's the place you ought to be, so they loaded up the truck and they moved to Beverly.

Karen. The reason I don't have a car is that it is so hard to find parking.

GREG A. I'd just rather walk.

TED. At least you can walk.

GREG A. Shut up, I know.

CHORUS. ...hills that is...swimming pools...movie stars. *(Musical end with jig and whups.)*

CURTAIN

STOMPING GROUNDS
©1992 by Spencer Kayden

(Spencer rides her bicycle very slowly around the stage.)

SPENCER. I'm nine years old. In my bare feet. Walking across our once cream now taupe shag carpeting and OW shi-, son of a bi—, god da—... and I don't even have to look down. I know what it is I stepped on. It's a Monopoly house. Jammed in between my two biggest toes. I shake it loose and leave it there for one of my brothers. I hobble into the garage and my limp down the street is just one big double-take — constantly mistaking bottle caps for quarters. Quarters, those 25 cent tickets to ride send me straight to the Ice Box Arcade. Four pieces of Grape Hubba Bubba and Jungle Hunt. Spearmint Bubblicious and Frogger. Original flavor Bubble Yum and Centipede and I'm set. And the ground there is littered with sweaty Red Hots and empty Lick-Em-Stik bags. *(Pause)* I don't recognize what's on the ground anymore. Is that a pinecone or a toy hand grenade? Is that spilled raspberry cranapple grape guava nectar juice or a blood stain? I don't know. And I think back to a time when I knew what my environment consisted of.

CURTAIN

STORY # 423
©1992 by Dave Awl

(The theater is dark. A spotlight clicks on to reveal Dave Awl standing center stage clutching three balloons to his chest.)

DAVE. A friend of mine got on the el train the other day and a man was sitting there holding a large balloon in his lap. The man himself was paying no attention to the balloon, but everyone around him was staring at it intensely. It was like they were fascinated by it, like they couldn't take their eyes off of it. Finally the man spoke. He said: "You can all go fuck yourselves. Quit looking at my fucking balloon." The people looked at the floor. The train stopped and the man got off. Two stops later a woman got on carrying a tank with a small lizard. Everybody very conspicuously avoided looking at the lizard. After a few minutes of this the woman lifts up the cover of the tank and the lizard says, "Jeez, relax, wouldja? It's not like I'm a goddamn balloon."
(The spotlight clicks off.)

CURTAIN

THE STORY OF X Y Z
©1991 by Karen Christopher

ADRIAN. Hey, what have you got?

PHIL. If I were you I'd check out that guy over there!

TED. Hey don't look at me, look at yourself for once. What have you got?

ADRIAN. Don't look at me, I'm not the one.

PHIL. Oh yeah that's what they all say, how come you were so quick to ask?

TED. Just throwing the blame that's what I say.

ADRIAN. Hey, you never answered my question.

TED. Hey you never asked me.

PHIL. You never asked him.

TED. You asked him but you never asked me.

PHIL. Not directly, you never asked directly.

TED. What do you want to know, go ahead, ask me.

PHIL. Ask him.

TED. Come on.

ADRIAN. WHAT HAVE YOU GOT?

TED. Nothing.

PHIL. Me neither.

ADRIAN. Oh, I thought I was the only one.

CURTAIN

STRANGERS IN THE NIGHT
©1990 by Phil Ridarelli

(Phil and Lisa are standing on stage. After a few moments Phil speaks.)

PHIL. It's getting warmer.

LISA. Yes. It is. *(Pause.)*

PHIL. Have you been here long?

LISA. No. Not really *(Pause.)*

PHIL. You should be careful around here. By yourself.

LISA. I'm fine thanks.

PHIL. An attractive woman. *(Pause.)*

PHIL. I'm sorry. I don't mean to bother you. I just want to talk to someone. Be close to someone. You don't want to talk? You too good for me? Look at me. Look at me, bitch. Touch me. Why don't you touch me, you fucking cunt?

(Lisa screams. Greg A. runs on, Phil flees.)

GREG A. Hey! What the fuck? *(to Lisa)* Are you all right? Did he hurt you?

LISA. Oh my god, I didn't do anything, he just started talking to me and the next thing I knew, he was yelling and, Jesus Christ...

GREG A. Shhh. O.K. It's o.k. You gonna be all right? Why don't I walk you home?

CURTAIN

STRETCH IT INTO OVERTIME
©1992 by Spencer Kayden

(Spencer and Greg Kotis stand facing each other. Phil stands between them holding a referee's whistle.)

GREG. Would this be an okay time to talk?
SPENCER. *(Looks at the clock)* Um...yeah, this is fine. Sure.
GREG. I just feel like we're both really busy and the only time I get to see you is when we're both here.
SPENCER. That's true.
GREG. I mean, I'm not a priority to you. You like your friends more than you like me. You don't care about me. You don't think about me enough. You'd rather be anywhere but with me. *(Phil blows his whistle.)*
PHIL. *(Gesturing referee style)* Making huge assumptions about the other person's feelings!
GREG. Do you see a problem in our relationship?
SPENCER. I don't know. *(Phil blows his whistle.)*
PHIL. *(Gesturing referee style)* Avoidance!
SPENCER. Well, yes. I feel like you expect more time from me than I can give you right now.
GREG. If you really loved me you would want to spend more time with me. *(Phil blows his whistle.)*
PHIL. *(Gesturing referee style)* Imposing your definition of love on the other person! Five yards. *(Greg steps back five yards. Phil points to Spencer.)*
SPENCER. You're a very needy person. *(Phil blows his whistle.)*
PHIL. *(Gesturing referee style)* Projection!
SPENCER. You know I care about you a great deal. *(Phil blows his whistle.)*
PHIL. *(Gesturing referee style)* Saying what you know the other person wants to hear!
SPENCER. Okay, remember when Holden Caulfield was... *(Phil blows his whistle.)*
PHIL. *(Gesturing referee style)* Literary reference!! 10 yards!
SPENCER. *(Spencer steps back ten yards.)* What do you have to say?
GREG. For every person there is a best person. And part of someone's being your best person is your being your best person's best person. *(Phil blows his whistle.)*
PHIL. *(Gesturing referee style)* Intellectualizing! Assuming love holds to a predetermined model or theory!
GREG. I just really really want to be with you. *(Phil blows his whistle.)*
PHIL. *(Gesturing referee style)* Stating the obvious! Simplifying the issue! Half time. *(Spencer retreats upstage to whisper with Ayun. Greg stays where he is. Phil whistles to signify end of half time. Spencer returns.)*
SPENCER. Your need for attention and affection from me, feelings to which you have a right and I in no way mean to belittle, is exacerbated by my current need for independence at this juncture in my... *(Phil blows whistle.)*
PHIL. *(Gesturing referee style)* Using prepared speech.
GREG. You are so selfish with your time. *(Phil blows his whistle.)*
PHIL. *(Gesturing referee style)* Stating your opinion as fact! Five yards! *(Greg backs up.)*
SPENCER. I just need you to need me less. *(Phil blows his whistle.)*

PHIL. *(Gesturing referee style)* Asking for fundamental change.

GREG. I swear I won't ask so much of you. *(Phil blows his whistle.)*

PHIL. *(Gesturing referee style)* Promising fundamental change!

SPENCER. I shouldn't ask you to change.

GREG. No, it's okay. I should change. I want to change. I've been working on trying to change. *(Phil blows his whistle.)*

PHIL. *(Gesturing referee style)* Grovelling!

GREG. Just tell me that you want this to work out. We're going to be all right, right? That's all I need to hear. Just so I know that you want to be here. Okay? *(Pause.)*

SPENCER. Okay.......fine. *(Phil blows his whistle.)*

PHIL. *(Gesturing referee style)* Agreeing with anything just to end the discussion.

GREG. Well, great.

SPENCER. Yeah. *(Pause.)* *(Phil looks back and forth waiting for the next move. He whistles.)*

PHIL. Game called due to indifference. A rematch will be scheduled for 2 months from today. Good game. *(Greg and Spencer jog towards each other, meet center stage and shake hands.)*

GREG & SPENCER. Good game.

CURTAIN

TAKE OFF YOUR SHIRT
©1990 by Karen Christopher

(Phil and Karen face each other, standing very close, looking into each other's eyes.)

KAREN. Here, let me iron your shirt. *(They break, he takes off his shirt...she begins to iron.)*

KAREN. The strangest thing happened to me the other day. I was walking to the el and a squirrel ran up to me like it was going to attack and then he followed me for several blocks.

PHIL. I wanted to tell you that I love you, but when I looked at you there were snakes sprouting off of your head.

KAREN. I kept trying not to look but I could hear his little claws scuffling down the sidewalk.

PHIL. I wanted to say that I would miss you when you go, but I looked at your feet and I saw hooves there.

KAREN. I was terrified. I knew it was silly but I was terrified. I looked over my shoulder and there he was.

PHIL. I wanted to tell you that I find you very beautiful, but I felt your hands grow rough and thick around my neck like the roots of a tree.

KAREN. I started walking faster but I could still hear his nails on the pavement. And I thought: this squirrel's really gone over the deep end.

PHIL. I saw you from across the room. You were stirring a pot on the stove. I imagined coming over, putting my arms around you and just holding you while you stood at the stove. But I realized you were cooking lizards and ringworm and lice.

KAREN. Then the steps were louder and heavier and they were going to overtake me. I turned around in a frenzy. It was a man and he was minding his own business on his way to work. But then I looked past him and there was the squirrel sitting in the middle of the sidewalk a little ways back.
(TOGETHER)

KAREN. If you had been there I wouldn't have been so frightened. I'm never afraid when I'm with you.

PHIL. You look fine now, though. I could say anything... *(They look at each other.)*
(TOGETHER)

PHIL. Huh?

KAREN. What?

CURTAIN

T.A.T.T.M.Y.C.
(THESE ARE THE THINGS THAT MAKE YOU COOL)
©1987 by Dave Awl and Ken Klawitter

(Dave, Phil, and Greg Allen stand rigidly facing the audience: feet apart, chest out...like robots or a new wave band. Throughout the piece, they move in a stiff, robotic fashion and speak in a nasal, staccato voice reminiscent of DEVO or the B-52's.)

DAVE. These are the things that make you cool!

PHIL. Shave the sides of your head!

DAVE. Dump some bleach on your jeans!

GREG. Write the names of musical groups you admire on your tennis shoes!

ALL. These are the things that make you cool! *(Dave, Phil, and Greg jump up and down three times in unison.)*

PHIL. Wear Grateful Dead paraphernalia even though you don't listen to them!

DAVE. Wear black on the outside, 'cause black is how you feel on the inside!

GREG. Rip holes in your pants so the world can see your knees!

ALL. These are the things that make you cool! *(They jump up and down three times in unison.)*

PHIL. Paint harsh words on the back of your leather jacket!

DAVE. Get your ear pierced - - but make sure it's the left one!

GREG. Say "I'm thinking of starting a band!"

ALL. These are the things that make you cool! *(They jump up and down three times in unison.)*

PHIL. Tie a piece of brightly colored string around your ankle!

DAVE. When discussing music, say, "I used to like their old stuff, but they're too popular now!"

GREG. Tie a bandanna on your head like Aunt Jemima! *(Each leans back to lift his right fist in the air.)*

DAVE. Dye your hair black to prove you're serious! *(They drop their fists.)*

ALL. These are the things that make you cool!

(In unison, Dave, Phil, and Greg jump up and down three times, spin to face away from the audience, and spin to face the audience again. They lean back to lift their right fists in the air.)

CURTAIN

THESE BOOTS ARE MADE FOR WALKIN'
©1990 by Lisa Buscani

(Lisa stands before the audience.)

LISA.
Fascism begins early
and small.
It has through the years
been enhanced and exaggerated
to the dark drama of cruel boots
crushing small, brave movements.
But in fact
its workings are subtle.

I met my destined rendezvous with fascism
in Mrs. Emory's fourth grade class.
Gloria Emory was a perky girl.
Her powder blue eyeshadow
smoked up to brown-penciled brows
Her polyester pantsuit
cuffed cleanly above
ding-dong ditchy, witchy black heels.
She was Nancy Sinatra with half the attitude
and a little less thigh.

She was neat
All the kids said she was neat.
SHE said she was neat,
and she expected everyone else to be neat, too.
And so, in an attempt to enforce
her iron-heeled, angora-covered
vision of neatness,
Mrs. Emory
would knock over and dump out
any desk that didn't match her standards.

Any desk.
Every desk.
Usually, my desk.

I didn't understand it.
I had order.
A lovably, eccentric bit of chaos
slap-dashed with a bit of pre-artistic frenzy;
a loony, loopy, goony, goofy,
head-in-the-air,
mind-in-the-clouds,
dog-ate-my homework kind of sensibility.
It worked for me.

I got stuff done,
I got my A's
my work was mine.

And as I bent down to gather
and smooth my interrupted structure,
I wondered:
Where was the respect for my spark?
Where was the willow's tension?
Where was the wisdom
that would hold my decisions at an arm's length
and see them for what they were?

I dream sometimes.
I dream of reaching back and standing tall.
I dream of rising above
the mark of the arbitrary hand.
I dream of wresting away
the yoke of the thick-tongued minion.
I dream of stepping proudly outside
lines and plans.
I dream of rising to the fullness
of my four-foot-eleven frame,
cocking back solid on my heels,
burning up at that Maybelline-clotted eye,
that lemon-curdled Jean Nate-face,
the sterile wind
of a two, two, two-mints-in-one-mouth
and saying
Bitch
If you touch my desk again,
I will rip out your uterus
and spare future generations
the terror of your spawn.

But I wake.
I wake and I find myself bending
to the same small issues
from the same small minds
in the same shamefully small world.
I wake
and it's cold
and every pencil has a point.
He called at twelve-oh-one,
the meeting is at three,
I saved the receipt,
the paper is white.

I wake
and I dream
of the fire
of chaos.

CURTAIN

THREE GUYS AND A DOLL
©1989 by Greg Allen

(Melissa holds up a small rag doll to the audience.)

MELISSA. This is an inanimate object. Its eyes cannot see, its stuffing cannot feel, and its joints move in both directions.

(Melissa walks off and hands the doll to Karen who cradles the doll in her arms and walks on cooing and cuddling it and talking to "little Joseph". She places the doll in a basket on a table and tucks him in, all the while telling him to be good and go to sleep. She says that he should just stay there while she goes into the next room. She exits. Greg, Phil and Randy enter from opposite sides of the stage throwing a softball to each other and making a lot of noise. After numerous tosses the softball "accidentally" slams into the basket and knocks the basket and the doll onto the floor. They suddenly stop making noise and apologetically go to see what they have done. Phil goes to pick the doll up off the floor but accidentally kicks it across the stage. He is regretful. Greg goes to pick up the doll but inadvertently steps on it as he does so. He tries to ease the injury he has done but slowly starts swinging the doll around by one arm, says "Doppler Effect" and makes the sound of a child crying in the Doppler Effect. He flings the doll to Randy who tells Phil to go out for a pass and throws it to Phil who shouts "Touchdown!" and spikes the doll. He then yells "All Star Wrestling!" and gets down on the floor and starts grappling with the doll until it has pinned him. Randy shouts "Body Slam!" and body slams his entire weight onto the doll. He throws the doll to Greg who shouts "Baseball!" and pitches the doll into Randy who hits the doll with his fists and then runs the bases as the other two field the doll and throw it into home plate while Randy slides into it. Phil grabs the doll and avidly slams its head in a locker door and flings it into the locker and closes it. The three guys leave laughing and whooping it up. Karen enters and discovers that "little Joseph" is not in his basket. She finds him in the locker and scolds him for being naughty and places him back in the basket saying "Now I told you to stay here and I meant it." Karen exits. Melissa enters, picks up the doll and says:)

MELISSA. This is an inanimate object. Its eyes cannot see, its stuffing cannot feel, and its joints move in both directions.

CURTAIN

TITLE
©1989 by Greg Allen

(Greg and Melissa sit at a table.)

GREG. Statement. Statement. Statement. Question?
MELISSA. Agreement.
GREG. Reassured statement. Confident statement. Confident statement. Overconfident statement.
MELISSA. Question?
GREG. Elaborate defensive excuse.
MELISSA. Half-hearted agreement.
GREG. Insecure statement. Distracted statement. Absurd statement.
MELISSA. Clarification question?
GREG. Panicked bullshit explanation! Quick meaningless comic non sequitur.
MELISSA. Laughter.
GREG. Fake laughter.
MELISSA. Laughter.
GREG. Fake laughter. Unconscious compliment of physical characteristics. *(Pause as he realizes what he's said.)*
MELISSA. Pleased response.
GREG. Shocked continuation of meaningless comic non sequitur.
MELISSA. Laughter.
GREG. Relieved confident laughter.
MELISSA. Laughter. Superficial compliment.
GREG. Self-assured agreement as denial. Exaggerated statement. Exaggerated statement. Grossly exaggerated statement.
MELISSA. Clarification question?
GREG. Extremely exaggerated elucidation.
MELISSA. Mental compliment with accidental double entendre.
GREG. Confident laughter.
MELISSA. Embarrassed laughter.
GREG. Confident laughter. Confident suggestive proposition?
MELISSA. Violent denial.
GREG. Aghast repetition as question?
MELISSA. Disgusted violent denial.
GREG. Defensive incriminating implication.
MELISSA. Offended retort.
GREG. Aggressive childish insult.
MELISSA. Disbelieving rhetorical question.
GREG. Aggressive childish insult.
MELISSA. Stunned silence.
GREG. Aggressive childish insult!
MELISSA. Defensive childish response!
GREG. Aggressive childish insult!
MELISSA. Defensive childish response!
GREG. Aggressive childish insult!

MELISSA. Defensive childish response!

GREG. Attempted Condescending Conclusive Statement! *(He begins to get up to leave.)*

MELISSA. *(Rising)* Brilliant Scathing Remark With Literary Allusions And Long Term Devastating Scatalogical Implications! *(She exits.)*

GREG. Pathetic self-revelation.

CURTAIN

T.O.T.I.
©1992 by Phil Ridarelli

(Tim and Ayun are on stage.)

AYUN. Well, Tim, it's time for me to leave the ensemble. I've obviously spent too much time with the Neo-Futurists.
TIM. What are you talking about? How can you say that?
AYUN. I went to see a play last week and I hated it.
TIM. What's wrong with that?
AYUN. It's a play that's been running on Broadway for months, making hundreds of thousands of dollars, and winning countless awards. I was surrounded by hundreds of people who loved it. I'm obviously not a good judge of theatre any longer.
TIM. Oh, Annie, there's no need to worry. You just need a refresher course in how to watch and appreciate theatre.
AYUN. Is there such a thing?
TIM. Sure, Annie, the Neo-Futurist Theatre Obedience Training Institute, founded as the Siddown and Shuddup School of Theatre Observation in 1925.
AYUN. Gee, Tim, tell me more about it.
TIM. Well, Ayun, TOTI offers you a 6-week comprehensive audience training program culminating in a group theatre outing, where you can practice the skills you've learned.
AYUN. Gee, sounds expensive.
TIM. You get the 6-week course plus the theatre tickets all for the low cost of $75.00.
AYUN. Wow! That's less than most theatre tickets alone. What does the training program consist of?
TIM. Well, let's peek into one of the classes.
PHIL. *(to audience)* The costumes *(they repeat after him)* revealed the characters...in ways I never dreamed possible.
TIM. This class is learning how to discuss theatre.
PHIL. Andrew Lloyd Weber's music... revealed the characters... in ways I never dreamed possible. Good! David Mamet... is a fucking poet. *(Greg A. walks onstage and takes a bow.)*
BETSY. No! NO! He's a star, dammit! He's the man you've come to see! Now let's let him know how we feel about him. *(Greg reenters. Audience responds)*
BETSY. Better. Now, listen the standing O is a tricky maneuver. I don't want you people jumping ahead of the game here. All in good time.
TIM. You'll also learn when to laugh, when to cry, and what to wear to the theatre.
AYUN. Boy, Tim. I can't wait to get started. What's the theatre outing for this semester?
TIM. Well, this week we can see Marlo Thomas in *"Six Degrees of Separation"* or Greg Brady in *"City of Angels."*
AYUN. Boy, it'll be just like watching T.V.
TIM. That's right! *(Ayun claps and barks like a seal. Tim feeds her a tasty little treat and pats her head.)*

CURTAIN

TRAPS
©1992 by Heather Riordan

(Heather sits in the audience and delivers the following text.)

HEATHER. Yes, I saw it—I saw a mouse. The mouse ran across my tiled bathroom floor—maybe trying to be discreet, maybe trying to scare me, but its little claws clicked against the cold white floor. The mouse was long and thin and there was nothing remotely cute about it.

Here is why I fear the mouse. It is small. Very small. I know it is irrational to be afraid of something that is 5 times smaller than the amount of cellulite on my right thigh, but, you see, a larger animal would be all right. If there was an alligator or a grizzly in the apartment, I could see it and know it was there and say "don't go in the bathroom, there's a big fucking bear in there!"

But I can't do that, it's too small. Don't tell me to trap it, they never fall for that, and even if it did, the others would see what I've done and plan their revenge while I cleaned up splattered mouse brains. Because for every 1 you see, there's 15 more. And any action could trigger some violent swarm against me—a sea of creepy little disease-infected vermin out for my blood.

And they could be anywhere. They could be hiding under your pillow. They could be right about to scurry up your pant leg. *(screams)* They could be anywhere at all.

CURTAIN

TROLLER
©1989 by Lisa Buscani

(Phil, Adrian and Greg A. sit on stage. Karen walks by and they begin to hassle her. The hassling is crude and not good natured. Ayun walks by, and she is harassed. Lisa walks by, is hassled, turns and looks at the audience.)

LISA.
The wife's not home,
or the wife's not,
or he's a blue, blue boy
with a wet, eclectic mouth,
or just can't stand to hear himself
slam back like that,
or they're all, they're all,
well
they are.

And that's fine.
Hell, a spasm is the next best thing
to actually being there.
But you forget, I'm here.
Not pious per se,
but much too confused
by the politics of gift
to benefit from cold reality
of cash.

Please excuse the noise
which garbles out as anger.
I know that strangled hormones
can transform bare face and sweat pants
into baby's delight.
But you see
nobodies
every day
score points on me.
Heavy-handed, thick-tongued half shells
whose glazed eyes
I can honestly stare into and say
oh, fuck you.
This is my day
my time
my step fuller,
my mind leaner,
my mouth
the best of every goddamn thing you know.
These assholes are winning.
And the chance to say no
to an unconsented squeal

to an unsolicited bend and spread
is a little victory
that I will have.

So strip your gears
and anything else you damn well please
but this ample curve and flawed gate
walk where they will.
These hands wrap their magic
around the freedom of choice.
The choice is made,
the answer's no,
fuck off.
(Lisa leaves stage. Phil, Adrian, and Greg A. watch her leave.)
PHIL. Bitch.

CURTAIN

TRUE TORCH SONG
©1990 by Ayun Halliday

(Ayun sits in a chair made of Greg Allen and Phil's interlocked arms. Karen and Ted blow cigarette smoke from the floor. Spencer applies tears to Ayun's eyes with a turkey baster.)

AYUN. *(sings)*
WHEN I THINK OF YOU
AS I OFTEN DO
THERE'S A TEAR IN MY EYE
WATCH ME SHIVER AND SIGH, AS I SAY

(Speaks) Jesus Christ, what an asshole.

(Sings) NOW I'M ALL ALONE
SEEMS LIKE LOVE HAS FLOWN
AND YOU'VE TAKEN THE BED
I'M IN OVER MY HEAD, AS I SAY

(Speaks) That traitorous little pissant, that miserable shit sucking worm!

(Sings) YOU'VE GOT SOMEONE NEW
NOTHING I CAN DO
DON'T WORRY, BABY, I'M FINE
BUT WE WOMEN MUST PINE
AND I SAY
EVERYDAY

(Ayun hops out of the boys' arms for this upcoming rant.)

Listen, BoBo, you and your self-proclaimed feminist girlfriend make me want to puke with your pathetic display of cowardly deceit. First you told me there was no one else, then you told me you loved me, then you told me it was no one I know, but it turns out it's your best friend's girlfriend and all four of us work in the same restaurant. I hope you find time for self-reflection, locked in a closet feeling nothing but pain, twenty-four hours a day for three months. I hope she smothers you with her big fat ass!

(The boys scoop Ayun back up, much smoke and tears.)

(Sings) I'LL NEVER FORGET YOU-OO-OO.

CURTAIN

23 X

©1990 by Karen Christopher

PHIL. You don't want to hear it — do you — do you want to hear it?

HEATHER. One of the attending female guards threw up and had to be taken from the room.

TED. What if the Soviet Union said to Americans "We won't negotiate until you improve conditions for political prisoners now serving time in federal prisons."

LISA. Never happen.

ADRIAN. What's a political prisoner?

GREG A: Given a harsher than normal penalty for their crimes because of their political beliefs.

SPENCER. Blacks in the U.S. go to prison at almost twice the rate of Blacks in South Africa.

DAVE. What is sensory deprivation?

PHIL. Everything is painted white and black. The lights are always on. Do you want to hear more?

HEATHER. There is no human interaction, there is no physical contact with anyone not employed in the prison system.

TED. Strip searches.

LISA. One of the attending female guards threw up and had to be taken from the room.

ADRIAN. Susan Rosenberg received a sentence of fifty-eight years, twenty-three times the sentencing guidelines for her offense.

GREG A. Two and a half years.

SPENCER. What was her offense?

AYUN. Convictions: 8 counts possession of weapons, identifications, and explosives.

PHIL. Was she going to bomb something?

HEATHER. Yes.

TED. For involvement with the United Freedom Front opposing U.S. government support for apartheid in South Africa and war on the people of Central America.

LISA. 58 years.

ADRIAN. A man who bombed an abortion clinic got 7 years.

GREG A. What were his beliefs?

SPENCER. How many years did Ollie get?

PHIL. What are his beliefs?

HEATHER. There's no interaction, there's no contact with anyone not employed in the prison system.

TED. Woken up every hour.

LISA. Is this an experiment?

ADRIAN. The only way you can begin to understand it is to go into your bathroom, lock the door, lie down in the bathtub, and stay there for three years.

GREG A. The government denies it.

SPENCER. Cavity search.

PHIL. Tell me more.

HEATHER. Find out yourself!

TED. Today there are more than 100 people locked up in U.S. prisons because of their political actions or beliefs.

KAREN. I'll keep bright my vision and never stop working until we've built that better day.

CURTAIN

UNCLE VODKA
©1990 by Greg Allen

(Greg Allen sits in a chair with a glass and a vodka bottle full of water. He is Vanya. Karen sits at his feet beside him. She is Sonia. On the other side of the stage sits Phil. He is Astrov. Next to him stands Ayun. She is Nanny. Greg fills a glass and chugs it down. No drunkenness is ever evident in the play.)

GREG. Life sucks.

KAREN. Oh don't say that, Uncle. So much of life lies ahead of you Ivan Petrovich Vionitsky.

GREG. Call me "Vodka."

(He fills another glass and chugs it down.)

KAREN. I know that right now life is a long, long succession of tormented days and tedious nights, but one day, one day Uncle, God will take pity on us and send us a new life that is bright and beautiful, and lovely.

GREG. You'll always be plain. Fuck off.

(He drinks another.)

PHIL. I lost a patient today. He died under the anesthesia. I'm so tired. I wonder if I meant to kill him? *(He pours a glass of water from his own vodka bottle and chugs it down. He looks at Ayun.)*

PHIL. God you're old.

AYUN. Would you like something to eat?

PHIL. Do you think they'll remember us a hundred years from now, Nanny, and speak well of us? Do think they will?

AYUN. *(Pause.)* Would you like something to eat?

PHIL. Yeah, I didn't think so. *(He fills a glass and guzzles it down. Lisa makes a sudden dramatic entrance upstage. She is Yeliena.)*

LISA. I am a very beautiful woman.

GREG. *(To audience)* I love her.

KAREN. *(Of Phil)* I love him.

LISA. *(Of Phil)* He's kinda cute.

PHIL. I'm kinda confused. *(Greg and Phil fill another glass and empty it in unison.)*

AYUN. Would anyone like something to eat? *(Greg, Phil and Ayun exit.)*

KAREN. You married my father so I hate you.

LISA. Let's make up.

KAREN. Okay!

LISA. We'll drink to our friendship!

KAREN. From the same glass! *(They pour a glass and guzzle it together. The next scene is played with alternating elation and depression by each of the women.)*

KAREN. *(Up)* Are you happy?

LISA. *(Down)* No.

KAREN. *(Down)* Me neither. *(Up)* Do you like the doctor?

LISA. *(Up)* Very much.

KAREN. *(Up)* I love him!

LISA. *(Down)* Oh. There's no happiness for me on this earth. *(Up)* I feel like playing something!

KAREN. *(Up)* Oh do! !

LISA. *(Down)* There's no piano.

KAREN. *(Down)* You can't. *(Up)* Do you think the doctor likes me?
LISA. *(Qualified)* You have beautiful hair.
KAREN. *(Down)* He doesn't know I exist.
LISA. I'll ask him.
KAREN. But what if he hates me?
LISA. Then he should leave.
KAREN. How sad. But at least I'll know!
LISA. Trust me.
KAREN. I will. *(Karen exits. Phil enters.)*
LISA. Do you love Sonia?
PHIL. No. I love you. *(They embrace. Enter Karen and Greg with a large vodka bottle, seeing Lisa and Phil.)*
KAREN & GREG. Fuck. *(Ayun enters and stands by the door.)*
LISA. *(Seeing Karen)* Well, I must go now. *(She pours herself a full glass, drains it, and exits.)*
AYUN. She's gone.
PHIL. I, too, must go. *(He fills a glass, empties it, and exits.)*
AYUN. He's gone. *(Greg sits in his chair and Karen takes the other one.)*
AYUN. *(To Greg)* Why do you always wear black? *(Greg glares at her.)*
AYUN. I'm gone. *(She fills a glass, drinks it, and exits.)*
GREG. *(Pouring out a handful of pills from a bottle)* I think I'll kill myself now.
KAREN. No Uncle, you mustn't. We must go on living. We shall patiently suffer the trials which Fate imposes on us; we shall work for others, now and in our old age. We will work hard with the hope that one day we shall know a life that is bright and beautiful, and lovely. Put the pills away. We must go on.
GREG. But how?
KAREN. We shall drink, Uncle Vodka, we shall drink.
(Greg puts back the pills while Karen pours herself a glass and then they drink simultaneously, she from the glass and he from the bottle. The curtain is called when he empties the entire bottle.)

CURTAIN

UNDERSTUDY
©1992 by Heather Riordan

(Everyone is onstage in a semi-circle around a podium, upon which rests a plate of cupcakes. Everyone reads from a script while holding a sword, dagger, etc.)

ALL. We are the Neo-Futurists!

HEATHER. (#1). Oh, shit, I really have to go to the bathroom. *(To an audience member)* Would you mind reading my lines for me—it's really easy. Just read the highlighted stuff and stand where I was with the sword.

AYUN. (#2). Yeah, you know, I'm about to pee my pants *(To another audience member.)* Would you just take this part for me? Just stand right there, you're reading this part—thanx a lot.

DAVE. (#3). Well, that messes up my part if Ayun's gone—could you do my role for me? You're third, just stand up there. Great, thanx.

LISA. (#4). Did I leave the coffee on? Would you cover for me while I'm gone? Your part is highlighted.

TIM. (#5). Shit, I left the door unlocked—read my lines for me—OK?

GREG. (#6). Hey Phil, let's go in the other room and do some male bonding.

PHIL. (#7). Good idea, buddy *(to audience members)* Do our parts, all right?

(The new cast of audience members is now onstage in a semi-circle with weapons held high in left hand)

ALL. We are the Neo-Futurists!

#1. I am 1

#2. I am 2

#3. I am 3

#4. I am 4

#5. I am 5

#6. I am 6

#7. I am 7

#1. And this is our theatre!

#2. We can do whatever we want.

#3. We control this play!

#4. Give us music! We want music! *(Victorious music begins.)*

#5. *(looking at the cupcakes)* Let's eat the props!

#6. There are only 6 cupcakes!

#7. Someone must die!

(#7 stabs the person to his/her left [#6]. As #6 is dying, he/she stabs the person to his/her left. As #5 is dying, he/she stabs the person on his/her left. This continues until #1 is dying, as #7 greedily shoves one of the cupcakes into his/her mouth. With his/her last bit of strength, #1 crawls over to #7, and kills him/her.)

CURTAIN

THE VERDICT
(for Rodney King)
©1992 by Greg Allen

(Greg Allen has an outstretched hand with a small object in it. His other hand is behind his back. Betsy stands next to him.)

BETSY. What's that?
GREG. What?
BETSY. That, in your hand.
GREG. Gee, I never noticed it before. You want it?
BETSY. Well isn't it yours?
GREG. Yeah, but you can have it.
BETSY. No, I wouldn't want to take something away from you ...
GREG. *(Overlapping)* No, I'm sure there's plenty for both of us. Go ahead.
(Betsy thinks about it.)
BETSY. No I can't. It doesn't belong to me.
GREG. Sure it does.
BETSY. It does?
GREG. Well no, it doesn't belong to you . But it's your right to have it.
BETSY. It is?
GREG. Especially you. Go ahead.
(Betsy thinks about it again.)
BETSY. What's in your other hand?
(Greg removes a hammer from behind his back.)
GREG. Oh. A hammer.
BETSY. What's it for?
GREG. Don't worry about it. Go ahead, take it. It's yours.
BETSY. You were going to hit me with that hammer.
GREG. No. There are laws to protect against that kind of thing.
BETSY. So you won't hit me.
GREG. Go ahead, it's yours.
BETSY. And you won't hit me?
GREG. Try me.
BETSY. *(Referring to the object in Greg's hand.)* But that's rightfully mine.
GREG. Yes.
BETSY. And I deserve it.
GREG. Yes.
BETSY. What about the hammer?
GREG. Oh that's mine.
BETSY. Can I have it?
GREG. No. I said it's mine.
BETSY. What if I take it away from you and beat the fuck out of you with it?
GREG. That would be wrong.
BETSY. *(Pointing to the object)* But that's mine.
GREG. Yes.
BETSY. What's the hammer for?
GREG. To protect you.

CURTAIN

WAITING ON GODOT
©1992 by Heather Riordan

(Dave & Greg A. are seated at a table. There is a vase on the table with a barren flower stem. Ayun is in the audience.)

AYUN. Act I. *(Heather enters.)*
HEATHER. Are you ready to order? The special tonight is turnips.
GREG A. I wanted carrots.
DAVE. *(Pause.)* Shall we go?
GREG A. *(Pause.)* Yes, let's go.
AYUN. Act II. *(Heather replaces barren flower stem with a stem with one leaf.)*
HEATHER. Are you ready to order?
GREG A. *(Pause.)* We're waiting.

CURTAIN

WATCH ME WATCH YOU
©1991 by Tim Reinhard

(Complete darkness. As the lines are said, two glowing red eyes light up and go off after the line.)

SPENCER. I'm watching you.
TED. You seem to be having a good time.
GREG A. And that excites me.
HEATHER. I enjoy watching you enjoy yourself.
TIM. I get to live my life vicariously through your adventure.
SPENCER. But it's not as good as it used to be.
TED. Something is changing.
GREG A. Something is different.
HEATHER. Watching life happen is no longer filling me up.
TIM. I no longer want to watch life.
SPENCER. I want to live life.
TED. I want to be you.
GREG A. And actually live my own life.
HEATHER. I will enjoy my life.
TIM. Because others will be watching me.
SPENCER. And they will be empty inside.
TED. Empty.
GREG A. And that excites me.
(Nine pairs of lights light up and approach the audience.)

CURTAIN

WHAT ARE WE DOING HERE?
©1990 by Karen Christopher

TED. I have a tenuous grasp on reality.
RANDY. What do you mean?
TED. I mean, I don't really believe what I see.
RANDY. What do you mean?
TED. I mean, sometimes I say to myself: This can't be happening — it is happening, but it can't be happening.
(Karen enters)
KAREN. Hi, what's going on?
RANDY. Not much.
TED. I don't know.
KAREN. What do you mean?
TED. I mean I don't know what's happening.
KAREN. Are you for real?
TED. Maybe not.
RANDY. He's just fucking around: He has a tenuous grasp on reality.
KAREN. Ohh. I've heard of that.
RANDY. You have?
KAREN. Yeah. Want to get a cup of coffee?
RANDY. Sure. *(Randy and Karen exit.)*
TED. What a nightmare.

CURTAIN

WHAT GOES AROUND
©1991 by Ayun Halliday

(The actors sit in a circle and speak with a quick, unemotional delivery.)

GREG K. We were war heavy this winter.
SPENCER. But now the war is over.
TED. And our troops are coming home.
PHIL. And we haven't thought about the war in a long time.
TIM. Because the war is over.
AYUN. And our troops are coming home.
GREG K. And we'll have a parade.
SPENCER. It's a good time to leave Iraq.
TED. No electricity.
PHIL. No fuel.
TIM. No medical supplies.
AYUN. No sewage processing.
GREG K. No safe water.
SPENCER. So you boil your water on a kerosene hot plate.
TED. And your baby knocks it over and is badly burned.
PHIL. No electricity.
TIM. No fuel.
AYUN. And the doctors in the hospital tell you there's no medicine for your baby.
GREG K. And the doctor tells you to bring water for your baby.
SPENCER. No safe water.
TED. And your baby's stomach swells up.
PHIL. No medical supplies.
TIM. And then he's gone like your brother.
AYUN. 150,000 soldiers killed in Iraq.
GREG K. And your mother.
SPENCER. An unknown number of women and children killed in the bombing of a bomb shelter in Iraq.
TED. And your friends.
PHIL. There are no phones.
TIM. There is no mail.
AYUN. How can you know?
GREG K. It's a good time to leave Iraq.
SPENCER. The war is over after all.
TED. And our troops are coming home.
PHIL. They'll see all our yellow ribbons.
TIM. They'll see how much we care.
AYUN. We'll have a parade.
GREG K. And then it's business as usual.

CURTAIN

WHAT THE FUCK IS THAT SUPPOSED TO MEAN?
©1992 by Heather Riordan

(Tim sits center stage drinking a cup of coffee. Heather and Lisa enter, cross upstage of him, and exit while Heather speaks.)

HEATHER. So there's this guy, you know, that you work with, but at a different branch. You know him well enough to, say, go out for coffee after work one day. So you ask about that, about the possibility of coffee, in what you hope is a casual, off-hand sort of way—I mean you have to work with people he works with, and you really don't know anything about this guy. He could have a girlfriend (although you don't think so); he could have some sort of dysfunctional long-distance relationship that he never talks about—hell, he could have a boyfriend for all you know—I mean what the hell do you know? And so you ask—trying desperately to sound off-hand, you inquire, with great casualness, about the possibility of coffee. *(Lisa and Heather stop just behind Tim.)* And he says:
TIM. That sounds good. *(They resume walking.)*
HEATHER. Which means...what?...That he's secretly had a crush on you and has been dreaming of this for weeks? Or the idea of coffee sounds good, say, as opposed to tea? Or maybe it just sounds good, those particular syllables in that order, the way you say it—it sounds good? I mean, what the fuck is that supposed to mean? And who's to say? Certainly not this guy. No, he seems to delight in giving mixed signals, in being vague, being unclear. My God, how could you go out for coffee (or any other beverage for that matter) with this man who entirely refuses to clue you in as to what's going on at all? You never speak to him again.

CURTAIN

YOUNG PERSON'S GUIDE TO SYNCHRONICITY
©1992 by Dave Awl

(The theater is dark. We hear a drumbeat, and a spotlight comes up to reveal Greg Kotis beating out a rhythm on a cardboard box. After four repetitions of the phrase, Dave's spotlight comes up center stage and he begins speaking in counterpoint to the drumbeat.)

DAVE. There was this man who lived in a house and this man who lived in a house lived with some cats and the thing about this man who lived with these cats was that he didn't live with one cat two cats or even four or five cats he lived in a house with 365 cats. And the thing about these cats was that instead of being named ordinary cat things like for instance Daisy or Tiger or Feedbag they each were named with a date, like for instance October the 3rd, or March 28th. And if you went over to his house you'd be sitting in a chair talking to him and a cat would jump in your lap and start to paw you and claw you like cats do when they think you're someplace good to sleep and you'd say hey, what's the name of this cat? And the man, the man would think for a second and then he'd tell you a date like for instance May 12th — and you'd look kind of freaked out because May 12th just happened to be your birthday. Only, it wasn't always your birthday, sometimes he'd say September 26th and you'd have to think for a minute to remember that was your parents' wedding anniversary, or August 4th which was the day Vance Williams fell off Mrs. Paluska's sail boat and died because his heart stopped. Only sometimes you couldn't remember that date at all so the man, the man would look at you and go and get a book off the shelf and say: *(A third spotlight reveals Ayun who reads from a book. She also speaks in counterpoint to the drum beat.)*
AYUN. "June 17th. Day you fell down in the swimming pool age 4 and developed your fear of the water. Reason you don't drink. January 9th. Day you figured out how to masturbate. November 26th. Day you realized you weren't the only one who had an unhappy childhood." *(Ayun's light fades out.)*
DAVE. And then the man would look at you like you were a diagram explaining how to fix a broken radio, sit back down, ask you what you planned to do with your life. And you, you'd look back down at the that cat like how could it possibly know what it knew, and its eyes would be blank-- *(Greg stops drumming, his light blacks out.)*
DAVE. Like 2 empty marbles. *(Dave's light blacks out leaving the theater entirely dark.)*

CURTAIN